Studying Psychology

Palgrave Study Guides

Teaching Study Skills and Supporting Learning   *Stella Cottrell*
The Student's Guide to Writing   *John Peck and Martin Coyle*
The Mature Student's Guide to Writing   *Jean Rose*
The Study Skills Handbook   *Stella Cottrell*
How to Write Better Essays   *Bryan Greetham*
The Postgraduate Research Handbook   *Gina Wisker*
Research Using IT   *Hilary Coombes*

www.palgravestudyguides.com

Studying Psychology

Andrew Stevenson

palgrave

First published 2001 by
PALGRAVE
Houndmills, Basingstoke, Hampshire RG21 6XS and
175 Fifth Avenue, New York, N.Y. 10010
Companies and representatives throughout the world

PALGRAVE is the new global academic imprint of
St. Martin's Press LLC Scholarly and Reference Division and
Palgrave Publishers Ltd (formerly Macmillan Press Ltd).

ISBN 0–333–91907–6

This book is printed on paper suitable for recycling and
made from fully managed and sustained forest sources.

A catalogue record for this book is available
from the British Library.

10   9   8   7   6   5   4   3   2   1
10   09 08 07 06 05 04 03 02 01

Printed in Great Britain
by Creative Print and
Design (Wales), Ebbw Vale

Contents

List of Boxes

Foreword

This book gives you precisely what it says in the title – a guide to studying psychology. This is an excellent way to advance your studies, and much better than just learning the contents of a massive textbook. You see, there is a lot more to success in psychology examinations than just being able to describe loads of psychological studies and theories. In fact, if you know too much psychological evidence then it can become quite difficult to figure out which bits to use and which bits to reject when you come to answer questions in the examination. You can end up spending half your time dithering over what to put in and what to leave out, and end up with no time to finish the essay.

This guide gives you some clear strategies for making the best of what you know. To do this you need to show the skills, other than knowledge, that are an important part of learning. These skills include analysis and evaluation; the skills of selecting the most important features of any argument, and of being able to comment on the value of the evidence. I have to say that these skills are difficult to develop, but when you learn the tricks of the trade you can demonstrate these skills at will, amaze your friends and dazzle the examiners.

This text is written in an engaging and readable style, and takes you through many of the important analytical and evaluative issues in psychology. It also gives you some handy hints on how to use these skills in examinations. If you want, you can read the text from start to finish, but that is not the only way to use the book. You can also pick out the bits you need when you need them. Maybe, for example, you need to write up a practical report very soon (i.e. yesterday), in which case, you don't need to read the first two chapters just yet. Go straight to Chapter 3 and sift through to the bits you want.

When you get the chance you might like to go to Chapter 5 to figure out what kind of learner you are. We all have our own styles of learning and the best way to be successful is to be honest with yourself and plan your work according to your strengths. Some people work best when they are under pressure, and so it is probably not worth starting a piece of work a month in advance because you will still end up doing the bulk of it the night before the deadline. Figure out your learning style and play to your strengths.

If you have an essay to write, then before you start have a look at Chapter 2 to check out the do's and don'ts of essay writing. It is surprising how many good students do not make the best of their knowledge and ability because they have not followed the basic rules of essay writing. You can also look in this chapter to see how your DRREEEEEAAAMSS can help you.

So, there you have it. Use this text to help you make the best use of your psychological knowledge. I think you'll find it is very helpful.

Philip Banyard

Nottingham Trent University

Preface: What *isn't* this?

What this *isn't* is a comprehensive psychology textbook, crammed to its rafters with information about all the key studies, theories and concepts you'll ever need to know to succeed at undergraduate level. True, it *does* detail some pretty famous, pretty notorious research – Stanley Milgram's study of obedience, Sigmund Freud's case study of the horse-phobic Little Hans. And true, it does take a detailed look at the nature of psychology and the questionable status of psychology as a 'proper science'. But by and large the aim here *isn't* to fill you full of factual *knowledge* about *the study of behaviour and experience*. For that, you'll need a textbook. And there are plenty to choose from.

Rather, what you're holding in your hand is designed to help you develop the necessary *skills* and *strategies* for studying psychology. The question being addressed here isn't 'How much should I *know* about psychology?' but 'What should I *do* to study psychology effectively?'

Whether you're studying psychology at A-level, Access or first-year undergraduate level, sooner or later your tutor will present you with a series of hoops. If you want to jump through them with confidence and style it won't be enough for you to simply know a hell of a lot about what you've covered on your course. You'll also need to be skilled in *writing psychology essays*, *planning and carrying out research*, *using statistics*, *preparing for assessments* and *making the most of your own style of learning*. All of these skills receive plenty of attention in this book. Add them to the *knowledge* you've accumulated on your course, and your experience of studying psychology at undergraduate level should not only be twice as enjoyable, but twice as effective.

So by all means make sure you have access to a good, comprehensive psychology textbook. You'll learn plenty from it. And treat this book as its companion. Use it to guide you through the hoops your tutor puts before you and to help you make the most of what you *know* about the studies, theories and concepts you cover on your course. And keep both books close at hand – you will find that they complement each other well.

Acknowledgements

Thanks to Dr Louise Walker, University of Manchester, for help with the writing of this book, especially with the statistical content. Thanks, also, to Jeremy Hopper of Aquinas College, Stockport, for support, advice and help in feeding Harry.

1 Doing Psychology: Learning a New Science, Learning a New Language

Learning about psychology is like learning a new language. As your course starts you'll be bombarded with a sackful of new words, plus some new meanings for old words. This opening chapter will prepare you for these changes to your vocabulary. It'll help you 'get by' in the first few weeks of your course. It'll also explain how these new words (and new meanings for old words) have helped psychology fight for its status as a 'proper science'.

► Proving

Speaking as a psychologist, can I ever say I've 'proved' anything, like proper scientists do?

A sure way of getting a frosty response from your psychology tutor is to claim that you've *proved* a theory or that you've *proved* your experimental hypothesis. As soon as you say you've *proved* anything in psychology – whether it's a theory or an hypothesis – you've dropped a clanger. You'll get blank looks all round, but you might not get a satisfactory explanation about why. So let's try and sort out the confusion.

We'll begin by looking at how psychology research gets started. Where do researchers get their ideas from? Well, more often than not, things start with an existing **theory**, part of which is in need of investigation. In psychology, as in the so-called 'natural sciences' (physics, chemistry, biology), a theory is **a series of interrelated statements**

which attempts to explain certain observed phenomena. In order to test a theory a researcher will set about testing any one of these interrelated statements by carrying out a piece of research. But before s/he carries out any research s/he'll probably have an idea about what the results of the study will be. S/he'll make a prediction, or **hypothesis**. A **hypothesis** is a **testable prediction relating to a statement taken from a theory**. Then s/he goes ahead and tests the hypothesis by carrying out the study.

Let's play that back in stages:

(1) find an existing theory;
(2) find a statement from it that requires investigation;
(3) construct a testable hypothesis relating to the selected statement;
(4) carry out research to test your hypothesis.

These are the first four stages of what's generally called **the Scientific Method** in psychology. And it's in stage (5) of this method that the confusion about proof generally arises. Let's say our researcher has carried out her study and obtained a set of results. What does she do next? Well, she's got two options.

Either her hypothesis was incorrect: it was not borne out in her results. In which case she has to conclude that her hypothesis, along with the theory from which it was taken, is false. She has to **reject** her hypothesis. This isn't the end of the world. She doesn't lose any Brownie points for this. All that happens is that her theory has to be **modified**, updated to accommodate these new findings. Alternatively, she may want to modify the method of investigation and carry out the study again, just to check the incorrectness of her hypothesis.

Or she may find that her hypothesis was correct. So what? Has she *proved* the theory correct? Not at all, because someone else could come along tomorrow and test another statement from the same theory (or even another hypothesis related to the same statement) and find their hypothesis to be incorrect – thus falsifying the theory. So let's keep calm.

Our researcher hasn't *proved* anything. She's **accepted** her hypothesis. She's **supported** the theory. But she hasn't **proved** anything. So the final stage of the Scientific Method looks like this:

(5) support or modify existing theory.

In fact, you could say that rejected hypotheses are more useful than accepted ones. After all, a rejected hypothesis leads to a change or modification in a theory, whilst an accepted hypothesis produces no such change. Hence the following statement from the philosopher of science, Karl Popper:

Science progresses by a process of falsification.

To demonstrate how all this works in practice we'll look at an existing theory. Let's use Festinger's theory of **cognitive dissonance** from 1959. Like all theories it's a series of interrelated statements about an observed phenomenon. The theory of cognitive dissonance is about what happens when we have to deal with two conflicting cognitions at the same time. Festinger defines a **cognition** as **an idea we have about ourselves or our environment**. At any one time we may be holding a number of cognitions, such as *I'm a married man* and *marriage is a wonderful institution* as well as *I think it's going to rain*. These are not especially engaging cognitions but it is quite conceivable that I could think all these three things at the same time. They don't get in each other's way. But what happens when two or more cognitions *do* get in each other's way? What happens if I have to cope simultaneously with the belief that *smoking is bad for my health* and the knowledge that *I've just bought ten Bensons*?

Festinger is particularly interested in how we feel when something we believe is in conflict with something we've said or done. Anyone who's worked in retail will probably identify with this kind of dilemma. How often, during the course of a working day, would you find yourself saying (of a horrible blouse) *Yes, madam, this is just what you're looking for* or (of a preposterous tie) *Oh, yes, it suits you, sir*. And how does it feel? Bad, says Festinger. It makes you feel anxious. And the name he gives to this particular type of anxiety is **cognitive dissonance**, which can be defined precisely **as a state of psychological discomfort experienced when an individual simultaneously holds two inconsistent cognitions**.

So what do I do with cognitive dissonance when I've got it? Naturally, I try to get rid of it. And a good way of reducing the unpleasant effects of two conflicting cognitions is to change one of them, get it to agree with the other one. And if one cognition is something I've *said* and one is something I *think*, the most convenient one to change is the one I *think*. After all, I can't *unsay* what I've already said. So an effective method of reducing my feelings of dissonance is to *change my beliefs to fit in with my behaviour*. Hence, my new belief might well become *Well, my uncle lived 'til he was 110 and he smoked three packets a day* or *I look cool with a Benson*.

So that's how Festinger's theory looks, in a couple of paragraphs. Let's see how it looks as a series of interrelated statements:

A   inconsistency between cognitions produces feelings of discomfort;

B   dissonance is unpleasant and the individual will try to remove it;

C   the individual will try to avoid situations that might produce dissonance;

D   the greater the conflict between two cognitions, the more pronounced the avoidance strategies will be.

This isn't an exhaustive list, but these four statements are a good summary of Festinger's theory. And now that we've got an existing theory we can use it to illustrate the Scientific Method in psychology, a method which progresses according to five well-established stages. Stage one is now complete: we've got the existing theory we need. Next we have to select one of the statements related to the theory, preferably one which we feel requires some investigation. I'm going to be bold and recommend that we select:

Statement B   dissonance is unpleasant and the individual will try to remove it.

Actually, I didn't select it at all. In 1959 Leon Festinger himself and his research associate James Carlsmith selected *statement B* and constructed a testable research hypothesis related to it, in line with stage three of the Scientific Method. To test their hypothesis they constructed an ingenious and now famous experiment, which I'm about to describe. So you'll have to wait a little longer to find out precisely what their hypothesis was.

It's fairly common for psychological researchers to design studies in which they deceive their participants. A popular deception is to have **a member of the research team pretending to be a participant**. These 'pretenders' are called **confederates** or stooges.

Festinger and Carlsmith's experiment employed precisely this kind of deception. The unsuspecting participants in their study were a group of male undergraduates, who were each given a 30-minute task to complete. This involved turning wooden pegs that were set out in a tray. Sounds boring. That was the idea – to induce a feeling of tedium in the participants. Next, each participant was asked to tell a 'fellow participant' (actually a confederate) that the task was 'interesting, intriguing and exciting'. In other words they were asked to make a statement which was in conflict with their belief that the task was boring. The aim of this was to produce a feeling of anxiety or cognitive dissonance in the participants, since they now had *two incompatible cognitions*. As a reward for doing this the participants were paid: one group received $1, another group $20.

We call the **different groups in psychology experiments – conditions**. So here we've got a $1 condition and a $20 condition.

How about that hypothesis?

Don't worry, it's on its way. The researchers thought that both the $1 condition and the $20 condition would experience feelings of dissonance. But which group would feel it most? The conflict between thinking *it was boring* and saying *it was interesting* would cause a high level of anxiety in the $1 condition, certainly. But in the $20 condition it was predicted that the feeling would be reduced because this group could tell themselves *don't worry, it's not so bad, I only lied because I was being well paid.* It was therefore predicted that this group would feel a *lesser* degree of dissonance.

So that's the hypothesis?

Sort of, yes, but here it comes in more precise terms. In the final phase of the study Festinger and Carlsmith asked the participants to tell *them* how enjoyable they'd found the peg-turning task. They asked them to rate their enjoyment level on a scale of 1 to 10. The higher the rating, the greater their feeling of enjoyment.

They wanted to know if either of the two groups had changed their belief about the task to fit in with what they had said to the confederate – as a method of removing their dissonance. After all, **statement B** says **dissonance is unpleasant and individuals will try to remove it**. And Festinger and Carlsmith say that the $1 condition will be feeling the greatest degree of dissonance. Consequently they predict that of the two groups, this $1 condition will be more likely to alter their belief about the boring task. They will therefore rate it as being more interesting, on a 1 to 10 scale, in this final phase of the study. And that's the experimental hypothesis. Put precisely, it looks like this:

Testable Hypothesis: The \$1 condition will rate the task as more interesting than will the \$20 condition.

To sum up, then, the researchers have created a situation in which there is a high level of dissonance in one group and a lower level of dissonance in another group, since both groups have a *belief* which is incompatible with something they've *said*. The researchers then tried to find out if the high dissonance condition would be more likely to alter their *belief* to fit in with what they had said, in order to reduce their anxiety levels.

And that's just what happened. The \$1 condition rated the peg-turning task as being 'not so bad', compared with the \$20 condition who stuck to their guns and rated it as 'extremely boring' – a situation which is roughly equivalent to the shop assistant who finishes up liking the goods she's trying to sell, in order not to contradict what she's been telling her customers. Hence the belief that *Well, it's not such a bad blouse after all.*

So it's good news for Festinger and Carlsmith. Well, fairly good news, anyhow. They've **accepted** their experimental hypothesis. And as for their theory? They've **supported** it. Their theory remains *intact*. It lives to fight another day, until someone else comes along and finds one of its statements to be false. Then they'll have to alter the theory. Or, to put it more positively, they'll have the opportunity to develop their theory.

So here's how Festinger and Carlsmith's research fits in with the five stages of the Scientific Method:

(1) the existing theory of cognitive dissonance (*theory*);
(2) dissonance is unpleasant and the individual will try to remove it (*statement*);
(3) the \$1 condition will rate the peg task as more interesting than will the \$20 condition (*hypothesis*);
(4) the experiment is carried out to test the hypothesis (*research*);
(5) cognitive dissonance theory is supported (*support*).

Before we leave the subject of proving theories, it might be worth pointing out that Festinger's is one of the more complicated theories in psychology, and his study is one of the most complicated experimental designs in psychology. So if you've coped with things so far you shouldn't have too much to worry about with what's to come.

▶ **Causing**

Speaking as a psychologist, can I ever say something has 'caused' something else, like proper scientists do?

Your days of claiming proof of theories and hypotheses now behind you, it's time to walk into another minefield: the use of the word *cause* in psychology, as in *increased crowding causes increased violent behaviour in female mice*. Statements like this should be made with caution. I won't say you should never make them but I do recommend that you think very carefully about a number of issues before you do. And it wouldn't surprise me if, after thinking about these issues, you decide to keep the word *cause* out of your vocabulary on the grounds that it's more trouble than it's worth. It's your decision. And it's a tough one. So to help you make it, this section will look at the reasons why this word is such a troublesome one for psychologists.

Let's take the claim that *increased crowding causes increased violent behaviour in female mice*. Exactly what's being said here? I'm suggesting a **causal** relationship between two **variables**. A **variable** is **something whose value changes over time**. So actually I'm claiming that *an increase in variable A, crowding, **causes** an increase in variable B, violent behaviour in female mice*. But what does it mean to say that a change in one thing causes a change in another? Well, for roughly a hundred years psychologists have been unable to agree about the precise meaning of the word **cause**. At different times it has meant different things to different psychologists, which is not especially helpful. So let's consider the two most common meanings that have been attached to it and see if we can clear up some of the confusion:

Meaning 1 *To say that A causes B means that A is **necessary** for B to happen.* In other words, unless you have a change in *variable A*, you won't see a change in *variable B*. And you won't see a change in *B* unless you have a change in *A*. So in order to produce an increase in the number of fights amongst your female mice you'll *have* to increase the crowding level.

Meaning 2 *To say that A causes B means that A is* **sufficient** *for B to happen*, meaning that a change in *variable A*, on its own, will produce a change in *variable B*. You won't need anything else. So all you need to do to increase the amount of violence is to crank up the crowding level. You don't need to do anything else.

Do these meanings work?

Well, there are certainly problems with them. Take **meaning 1** to begin with. It may be possible to demonstrate that under certain experimental conditions increased crowding will produce an increase in violent behaviour. But then again, increased temperature may have the same effect. Also, the time of the year. For example, female mice may become more aggressive in June. So to say that increased crowding is *necessary* for increased violence is clearly wide of the mark. A change in *A* may well produce a change in *B*, but that isn't to say it's *necessary* for that change. Other things could do it too. For the moment, then, we can agree with many contemporary psychologists when they say that **meaning 1** is not always reliable.

How about **meaning 2**? If an increase in *A* is *sufficient* for an increase in *B*, I should be able to *control* the level of violent behaviour in female mice simply by varying the level of crowding. Variations in crowding alone should be sufficient to produce these changes. But there is a problem here. Let's say I *can* control the level of crowding in a community of female mice. And let's say I *do* observe changes in levels of violent behaviour. What about those other variables that are varying at the same time? I mean those **variables that aren't being controlled**, things like room temperature, season, the diet and age of the mice. It may be that fluctuations in any of these so-called **extraneous variables** might be influencing violence levels as well as the level of crowding. This will interfere with my causal claim. I will have less confidence in my causal statement. So clearly there are problems with **meaning 2** as well.

So now what? Do we give up hope of using the word 'cause' in psychology?

No, wait. There may be a solution. After all, lots of reputable psychologists do look for causal relationships in their research. So presumably they must have found a way around *the problems with the two meanings of the word 'cause'*. How do they do it? Do they simply ignore them and plough on regardless? Well, no. Their way of dealing with *the problems with the two meanings of the word 'cause'* is to do all their research in one particular way and in one particular place.

When they carry out their research they use one particular **method**. A **method** is **a way of carrying out research**. And the chosen method of anyone who is trying to establish causal relationships in psychology is the **controlled experiment**. And the place they use to conduct them is the laboratory. In a **controlled experiment** the researcher **observes the effect of a change in the value of one variable on the value of another, whilst attempting to control all other extraneous variables**. Experimenters who use this type of method try to bring all those variables which they would otherwise be unable to control, under their control. So, for example, if I were to set up **a controlled experiment to investigate the relationship between overcrowding and the violent behaviour of female mice**, my design could be written out like this:

Step 1: select a sample of 40 female mice;

Step 2: record the age of each mouse;

Step 3: create two conditions, *X* and *Y*, with 20 mice in each condition;

Step 4: allocate an equal number of old and young mice to each condition;

Step 5: house *condition X* together in a small cage;

Step 6: house *condition Y* together in a large cage;

Step 7: record the number of violent acts per hour for each mouse for 48 hours;

Step 8: test both conditions in June;

Step 9: maintain the temperature in the two cages at an equal level.

The hypothesis for this experiment states that *condition X will display more violent acts than condition Y.* For the purpose of this discussion it is especially important to notice how many *extraneous* variables I've taken control of in the design of this experiment. These are variables that would be beyond my control if I were to conduct the study in a **naturalistic** setting (that means **outside the laboratory**, where participants are studied in their natural environment).

There are four such variables in my experiment: age, season, temperature, number of mice in each condition. Did you spot them? I've kept these variables equal, or constant, for the two conditions, *X* and *Y*. So if there does turn out to be an increase in violent behaviour in *condition X* I'll be in a stronger position to claim that it's due to the increase in crowding; rather than, for example, the fact that the average age for one condition was higher.

So what would be the outcome of an experiment like this? Well, for the sake of argument let's say that there *was* an increase in the level of violent acts in *condition X*. Just as I predicted. So now I can propose a *causal* relationship between an increase in *variable A* and an increase in *variable B*. I can go ahead and claim that a change in *A* caused a change in *B*. In doing so, remember, I'll be claiming that the change in *A* was **necessary** and **sufficient** for the change in *B*.

It was **necessary** because *in my experiment* no other variables were allowed to have any influence on the level of violent behaviour. After all, I had all those extraneous variables like age, season, temperature and number of mice in each condition, *under my control*. I held them constant for the two conditions. So, in my experiment, in order to increase these violence levels, an increase in the crowding level was *necessary*.

It was **sufficient** because in my controlled experiment crowding was the only variable that was allowed to have any effect on the level of violence. As I've just said, all the others were under my control. So in order to vary the violence levels all I had to do was vary the crowding levels. It was enough on its own.

Therefore, in my experiment, changes in variable *A* were necessary and sufficient to produce changes in variable *B*. To put it bluntly, they caused them.

So it looks like we can use the word 'cause' in psychology.

Well, not exactly. Whilst I hate to pour cold water on these enthusiastic claims about the apparent causal link between our two variables, *A* and *B*, I'm afraid there are a couple of problems here – a couple of problems that illustrate the reason why this word *cause* is so sparingly used in psychology.

Problem 1 *You can't control everything in controlled experiments*

Even though I made a fairly good attempt at controlling the extraneous variables of age, temperature, season and the number of mice in each condition in my experiment, there were some other extraneous variables I didn't control. In all controlled experiments, despite the meticulous efforts of researchers, there are always variables that *should have been controlled but weren't* – not simply because of carelessness, although this is sometimes the reason. More often it's because it is extremely difficult to create a truly controlled environment. For example, in my experiment what if *condition X* had been selected from particularly violent colonies? Or what if a *condition Y* developed an epidemic of mouse flu, or some other lethargy-inducing disease, during the course of the experiment? Or what if a high number of participants of *condition X* had an unusually high metabolism? I could go on but I won't. The point is that any of these uncontrolled extraneous variables might well have influenced one of my conditions more than the other, thus reducing the amount of control in my experiment. It is extremely difficult for researchers to control all possible extraneous variables in their experiments. And the ones they overlook will interfere with any causal relationships that may arise out of their work. This makes their use of the word *cause* less convincing.

Problem 2   *Ecological validity*
In my experiment I'm observing and recording the behaviour of the mice in their newly acquired cramped – or spacious – cages, depending on which condition they're in. I discover that the mice in the cramped cages are more violent than the ones in the spacious cages. All well and good. I accept my hypothesis. But at the back of my mind I have the feeling that I'm studying mice under *unusual circumstances*. They're in a new environment, with new peers, and a number of new tests have been run on them. Consequently it occurs to me that if they're anything like you or me they might *behave unusually* in such circumstances. This makes it harder for me to make generalisations from the results of my study about the natural, everyday behaviour of other mice, or indeed humans. And if mice behave unusually under controlled conditions I'm pretty sure that you or I would. So when humans are used as participants in controlled experiments it is even more difficult to translate the behaviour they exhibit in the laboratory into theories about everyday human behaviour and experience. Another way of putting this is that the results from controlled experiments lack **ecological validity**, meaning they lack **applicability to real-life settings**. So many psychologists are wary of claiming causal links between variables when these variables have been observed

and tested under controlled settings (that is, in controlled experiments). This makes these causal claims less convincing.

In summary then, you could say that psychologists face two problems when using the word *cause*. Firstly, there are so many extraneous variables that have to be considered when designing a controlled experiment that some are likely to be overlooked. And secondly, the more extraneous variables they *do* manage to control, the more difficult it is for them to draw conclusions about everyday behaviour and experience from their research. These problems reduce the validity of psychologists' claims about causal relationships.

Clearly, this 'c-word' is a difficult one. Is it best to avoid it? Is there another word that should be used in its place? Before we try to answer these questions, let's see how one particular researcher dealt with the problems of *causing* in psychology.

Stanley Milgram's 1963 study of obedience is famous for producing a surprising set of results and for sparking off a debate about whether researchers are within their rights to subject their participants to stressful situations in the interests of finding out more about human behaviour.

Milgram wanted to find out if people would obey an instruction even if it resulted in fatally injuring a colleague. Participants were drawn from a range of skilled and unskilled occupations. They responded to a newspaper advertisement requesting volunteers 'for a study of memory'. On the day of the experiment each participant reported to Yale University Psychology Department, where each was greeted by a lab-coated man in his thirties who then introduced them to Mr Wallace. Mr Wallace was a mild-mannered forty-something confederate who, in traditional style, was playing the role of another participant. The participant and Mr Wallace were informed that they would be working together on an investigation into 'punishment and learning' and that one of them would be assigned the role of 'learner' and the other one would be assigned the role of 'teacher'. Milgram saw to it that the participant always got the role of 'teacher'. What followed were unpleasant or titillating scenes, depending on your tastes.

Mr Wallace, by now strapped into a (fake) electric chair, was given a (fake) memory test in which he had to demonstrate to the 'teacher' that he had learned a sequence of words. The participant was instructed to give Mr Wallace progressively more intense (fake) electric shocks after each mistake he made. And Mr Wallace, obligingly, made plenty of mistakes. Each time a shock was administered the participant would hear (fake) screams of pain coming from the adjoining room, where Mr Wallace was sitting. Each time the teacher got squeamish and complained of not wanting to continue, the lab-coated official, who was standing only a few feet away from him, would issue verbal prods like 'please continue' or 'you must go on'.

Milgram wanted to find out how many of the 40 participants would follow the instructions up to the maximum reading on the (fake) voltage board, by which point Mr Wallace's screams had, rather ominously, faded to silence. The answer was 26 – a disturbingly high number, which doesn't inspire a lot of confidence in your fellow man (or woman, since not all of Milgram's participants were male). But it's what happened next that is of particular interest to us.

Clearly the participants who took part in this experiment had been shown to be an obedient lot. But *why*? What interested Milgram now was **what variable in the design of his experiment was the crucial one in producing such a high level of obedience?** He had a few ideas. So he made a shortlist list of them:

Idea 1   Was it the prestigious, academic nature of the Yale University setting?

Idea 2   Was it the fact that the 'teacher' couldn't see Mr Wallace during the experiment?

Idea 3   Was it the proximity of the lab-coated experimenter, who was right next to him, urging him on?

Idea 4   Was it that the 'teacher' was alone, with no one present to encourage him to quit?

To find out which of these four ideas was most accurate, Milgram designed a number of controlled experiments. For example, in order to investigate *idea 1* he replicated his experiment in a run-down office block whilst keeping all the other variables the same as in the original study. Under these circumstances the obedience level fell from 65 per cent to 48 per cent. This was still an alarmingly high number, suggesting that the so-called 'Yale factor' was not the crucial one.

In fact, the variable which seemed most responsible for the high level of obedience was the one associated with *idea 4*. The obedience level fell to 10 per cent when there was a second confederate in the room next to the participant, urging him to quit delivering the shocks. Milgram concluded that the absence of peer pressure, someone to look to for guidance (a so-called 'dissenting peer') was particularly influential in producing a high level of obedience in his original experiment.

The results for Milgram's four follow-up experiments are summarised as follows:

Experimental design	*Obedience level*
original experiment	65%
when the experiment took place in a run-down office block setting	48%
when the 'learner' was in full view of the 'teacher'	40%
when the 'prodder' was moved away from the 'teacher', into the next room	21%
when the 'teacher' was accompanied by a 'dissenting peer'	10%

Using the results of these four follow-up experiments, we can rank the four possible reasons for high obedience from the most influential one to the least influential one:

First   the absence of a dissenting peer.

Second   the presence of a lab-coated official standing in close proximity urging the participant to continue.

Third   Mr Wallace being in the next room and therefore invisible.

Fourth   the academic setting of Yale University.

Milgram's work shows that all four of these variables had some effect on the level of obedience. We can say this with confidence because in each of the four follow-up studies the level of obedience changed as each of the four variables was manipulated. For instance, when Mr Wallace was placed next to the 'teacher' and all other variables were kept the same as they were in the original experiment, the obedience level changed from 65 per cent to 40 per cent. But we *can't* say that any one of these four factors *caused* the increase in obedience levels. Why not? For the two reasons we discussed earlier. To illustrate these two reasons, let's take the follow-up study which dealt with the variable which was ranked as the *most influential*, the absence of a 'dissenting peer':

Reason 1: *You can't control everything in controlled experiments*

When Milgram conducted his experiment with a 'dissenting peer' standing next to the 'teacher', whilst keeping everything else the same as in his original experiment, obedience fell to 10 per cent. This suggests that the presence or absence of the peer *influences* the obedience level. But it would be too much to claim a *causal* relationship here. After all, there may have been other, uncontrolled extraneous variables also having an influence. For example, the original study and the follow-up study may have been held during different seasons. Or they may have been held at different times of day. Or during different political climates. Extraneous variables such as these, which were not held at a constant level over the two experiments, would make any causal claim less convincing.

Reason 2: *Ecological validity*
Although it appears that the absence or presence of the dissenting peer is an influential factor in this experimental demonstration of obedience, the fact remains that this demonstration took place under unusually controlled conditions – conditions that were far removed from the naturalistic, everyday conditions we are used to. It is difficult to confidently apply the findings gathered under such unusually controlled conditions to our everyday experience. This makes the claim that there is a *causal* relationship between the two variables less convincing.

All this suggests that to claim that the change in one variable (the appearance of the 'dissenting peer') *caused* the change in another variable (obedience) would be unwise and inaccurate. Nevertheless, it is clear from Milgram's experiments that there is some sort of connection between these two variables, maybe not a causal one, but a relationship which is more than just a *random* one. So if we can't be confident in calling it *causal*, what *can* we call it?

Well, the good news is that for those psychologists who have decided to avoid the 'c-word' when drawing their conclusions, there is an alternative, a word you can use without upsetting anyone. And it's another c-word. And the word is **correlation**.

Correlation: the other 'c-word'
The outcome of psychological research often leads researchers to conclude **that two variables alter their value at the same time**. In other words, they go up and down together. This is called a

correlation. In one experiment I observed that an increase in crowding was consistently associated with an increase in violence. The two varied together. Milgram observed that the absence of a dissenting peer was consistently associated with an increase in obedience. Again, the two varied together. We have suggested that in both of these cases it is dangerous to assume these variables are *causally* related. So let's ease off a little. Let's say instead that these are *correlational* relationships – relationships where one variable is seen as varying reliably, predictably and consistently at the same time as another, so that when a change in *variable X* is observed you can bet you'll observe a change in *variable Y* too. (Chapter 3 has a longer discussion of correlation and Chapter 4 will tell you more about the statistics associated with it.)

After all, in a world where we can't control all the extraneous variables in our experiments, there's no *need* for us to suggest that the changes in *variable X* are actually *causing* the changes in *variable Y*.

▶ Being right

Speaking as a psychologist, can I ever say something is 'right', like proper scientists do?

Another good way of giving your psychology tutor indigestion is to point to a theory (or a statement taken from a theory) and ask if it's *right*. You'll get the same reaction if you ask whether the conclusions arrived at by a particular researcher are *right*. Was Milgram *right* about obedience? Was Festinger *right* about cognitive dissonance? And what about a statement like *Women are more intelligent than men* – is *that* right?

Well the truth is when you use the word *right* in psychology you open up a can of worms that can be just as unpleasant as the ones you open up when you use the words *proving* and *causing*. Suggesting that a statement or conclusion is *right* is something psychologists do very cautiously. But there are circumstances under which they will do it. In this section we'll look at two sets of circumstances under which it's all right to point at something and say that it's *right*. But before we look at the first of these we're going to consider something beginning with 'E'.

Empiricism

If you were to argue that psychology should base its theories on *observable data* which has been gathered from research, rather than basing its theories on *discussions and arguments*, you'd be arguing an empiricist's viewpoint. Empiricism is a **philosophy which concerns itself with how psychology should conduct its research and draw its conclusions**. Empiricists argue that support for all theories (and all statements taken from theories) should be demonstrated *for all to see*, in research settings like laboratories, for example. In fact, they regard theories (and statements) that have no such support as *unscientific*. Theories that arise out of *discussions and arguments* alone are described by empiricists as 'armchair theories' and aren't taken seriously. The Scientific Method we discussed earlier in this chapter is central to the *empirical* approach to psychology.

So how does this help us?

Well, it may be that we can use the concept of empiricism to help us answer some of our queries about the *rightness* of theories and conclusions in psychology. To figure out how, let's take a closer look at the statement that made a brief appearance in an earlier paragraph:

> Women are more intelligent than men.

Let's call this *statement A*. And let's say that *statement A* is one of a number of statements that collectively form *theory A*, which states that:

> Intelligence is determined by gender.

Naturally, being psychologists, we'd like to test this theory. But because we've read the first part of this chapter we know that theories (and statements taken from theories) cannot be tested directly. We need a testable hypothesis relating to *statement A*. One possibility would be:

> A sample of 20 women will outscore 20 men on the Evans Intelligence Test.

Now we have the full set. A *theory*, a *statement* taken from it and a testable *hypothesis* relating to the statement:

> *Theory A*:   Intelligence is determined by gender.
> > *Statement A*:   Women are more intelligent than men.
> > > *Hypothesis A*:   A sample of 20 women will outscore a sample of 20 men.

Incidentally, none of these 'three As' actually exist in the form I've presented them. I've made them up for our present purposes, along with the *EIT*. However, the question of a link between IQ (intelligence quotient) scores and gender is a hotly disputed one in psychology.

But let's get back to our original question: *is anything ever right in psychology?* Here we have a theory, a statement and a testable hypothesis. And there you are in your psychology class with your hand in the air demanding an answer to your question 'Are any of these "three As" right?'

If your psychology tutor is in the mood to produce an informed, carefully thought out answer, it will go along these lines. She'll begin by reminding you that neither theories (nor statements taken from them) can be *proved* in psychology. They can be *supported* by the results of research, in which case they live to fight another day. And it only takes one set of research findings to *oppose* a theory (or statement) and it is *falsified*, leading to its having to be modified in some way. Therefore, according to the terms of the Scientific Method, we can say that theories and statements cannot be proved *right* but they can be shown to be false. In other words, they can be *wrong but not right*.

Pausing momentarily to allow this to sink in, she'll then go on to remind you that hypotheses have something that theories (and statements taken from them) don't have. Namely, *testability*. After reading a hypothesis a researcher should be able to go away and design a piece of research to test it. Hypotheses also *predict* the outcomes of research. And the accuracy of such predictions are demonstrated *for all to see* by the results of the ensuing study. If an hypothesis predicts the results accurately, the theory from which it was derived is *supported* and will live to fight another day. If it doesn't predict the results accurately the theory will have to be modified.

The key point here is that the accuracy, or *rightness*, of the hypothesis can be demonstrated *observably*. It can be demonstrated *empirically*. Before your very eyes. Another way of putting this is to say that hypotheses can be clearly shown to be *right or wrong*.

How does this relate to our 'three As'?

In the case of *hypothesis A*, if the sample of 20 women does outscore the sample of 20 men, the hypothesis is *accepted* as *right*. *Theory A* and *statement A* are then *supported* and live to fight another day. But if the female sample doesn't outscore the male sample, the hypothesis is *rejected* as *wrong* and *theory A* has to be modified.

So there you have it. One circumstance in which psychologists will say that something is *right* is when they're talking about **testable hypotheses**. **Box 1A** just about sums this up.

Box 1A   Can theories, statements and hypotheses be right or wrong?

	Can they be right?	**Can they be wrong?**
Theories	**No.** But they can be **supported** by research findings	**Yes.** It only takes one research finding to oppose a theory and that will show it to be false and in need of some modification.
Statements	**No.** But they can be **supported** by research findings. This produces support for the theory from which the statement has been taken.	**Yes.** One piece of evidence will show a statement to be false, along with the theory from which it has been taken. Modification will be required.
Hypotheses	**Yes.** Because they are **empirically testable**. They predict events that are observable. If hypotheses are right, the statements and theories they derive from are then supported.	**Yes.** If the event a hypothesis predicts does not transpire, it is wrong. So we reject it, along with the theory it comes from.

Are there any other circumstances in which psychologists will say something is 'right'?

Well, yes. Sort of. But before we consider these we're going to consider something beginning with 'P'.

Paradigms
'So what is psychology then?' 'And what do you actually *do* in psychology?'

If you enrol on a psychology course you'll have to get used to coming home from college and facing these two questions from your family, friends, lodgers, landlord, etc. If you'd chosen pharmacy, economics or aerobics you wouldn't have had this to cope with. And even if you had you'd have found a way to fob them off with a coherent response. The fact is, even professional psychologists can't agree on the answers to these two questions.

For the past hundred years there's been debate about what the subject matter of psychology is and about how to conduct research into it. To put it another way, psychology has lacked a **paradigm: an agreed definition of what is to be studied and how to go about studying it**. Instead, different groups of psychologists have co-existed, researching, forming theories, whilst having different ideas about *what* psychology is and *how* it should be studied. These groups are sometimes referred to as 'schools of thought'.

How does all this help us?

Well, it may be that we can use this concept of *paradigms* to help us discover another one of those rare circumstances under which psychologists are prepared to use the word *right*.

We'll return to this presently. First, take a look at **Box 1B**, which tells you more about some of the more influencial paradigms in psychology. These aren't all the schools of thought in psychology. There are seven or eight main ones.

At different times over the last hundred years particular schools have been more popular than others. During the 1920s, for example, behaviourism had its heyday. More recently the cognitive approach has been in favour. It comes and goes in cycles. The one constant factor is that no single school of thought has ever dominated psychology so much that the others have thrown in the towel and abandoned their own

Box 1B Different paradigms have different ideas about what psychologists should study and how they should go about studying it

Paradigms include . . .	Famous names include . . .	The subject matter of psychology is . . .	Psychology should be studied using . . .
Psychoanalysis	Freud Jung Erikson	. . . the **emotional** or affective aspects of human personality. In particular, how these aspects develop and how they are influenced by unconscious motives.	. . . **case studies** involving detailed, often prolonged analysis of an individual participant's ideas and memories.
Behaviourism	Pavlov Skinner Watson	. . . how **behaviours** are learned. The effect of the environment on this learning process, how we can control behaviour by controlling the environment.	. . . **experimental research** in controlled settings, such as laboratories. Such experiments often use non-humans as participants.
Cognitive Psychology	Piaget Gregory Broadbent	. . . **thinking**. In particular, memory, problem solving and visual perception. Also, how we develop and use our capacity for language.	. . . **experimental research** in controlled settings, such as laboratories. These experiments predominantly use humans as participants.

preferred ideas about *what* to study and *how* to study it. There's never been a single, dominant paradigm.

If you look closely at the three schools of thought in Box 1B, you'll see that each of them has an interest in a different aspect of 'the whole person'. They all have an interest in people, but for different reasons. If, for instance, you were to be studied by a psychoanalyst, s/he would pay particular attention to your *emotional* (sometimes called *affective*) life. A behaviourist, on the other hand, would focus on your *actions* rather than your feelings, that is, *what you do* rather than *how you feel* about what you do. And just to be different again, a cognitive psychologist would concentrate on your powers of reasoning and problem solving. S/he'd want to know about the *thinking* part of you, rather than the *feeling* and *doing* parts. Because of their special areas of interest, these three approaches are sometimes referred to as *The A (affective) B (behavioural) C (cognitive)* of psychology.

But let's get back to our central question. *Are any of these schools of thought right?* Well, it depends who you talk to. This might seem like a confusing answer, so let me try to explain it.

Put yourself in the position of a psychologist who has carried out a piece of research and drawn conclusions from the results. And for the sake of argument let's say you're a psychoanalyst. In other words you're from the psychoanalytic school of thought. You regard psychology as the study of *affective* aspects of 'the whole person'. You carry out research using individual *case studies* rather than large-scale surveys or experiments. In short, you use the psychoanalytic *paradigm*.

Now let's try that question again. Are the conclusions you've drawn from the results of your research *right*? Well, as I suggested a couple of paragraphs ago, it depends who you talk to. If you talk to another psychoanalyst your conclusions may well be regarded as *right*. If, on the other hand, you talk to a behaviourist (or a cognitive psychologist) your conclusions will almost certainly *not* be regarded as *right*.

In other words, if you talk to someone who shares your *paradigm* (your ideas about *what* psychology is and *how* it should be studied) they're likely to agree with the conclusions you've drawn and they may well regard them as *right*. Mind you, this isn't guaranteed. It's quite likely that even a fellow psychoanalyst who shares your *paradigm* will still disagree with your conclusions. Nevertheless, when you're talking to someone from your own school of thought there's a reasonable chance they will agree with you because they share your ideas about *what* psychology is and *how* it should be studied.

If, on the other hand, you talk to someone who doesn't share your *paradigm* (a behaviourist, for example) you'll find them reluctant to agree with your conclusions. Not only will they be unlikely to regard them as *right,* they may even draw their own, different conclusions from your results – conclusions that fit more closely with their own school of thought, their own *paradigm.*

To summarise, psychologists will be far more likely to regard the conclusions drawn from research data as being *right* if they share the *paradigm* of whoever carried out the research. To illustrate how this works in practice we'll look at Freud's 1909 case study of *Little Hans,* famously known as the 'Analysis of a Phobia of a Five-Year-Old Boy'.

Freud was the founder of the psychoanalytic school of thought. He carried out his research using individual case studies rather than large-scale surveys or experiments. But his research into the case of Little Hans was unusual in that the two only ever met twice. Consequently he gathered all his data by talking to and exchanging letters with the boy's father.

When Hans was four years old his father reported that his son had developed a fear of horses. In particular, he was afraid of 'horses falling down in the street'. This isn't as strange as it sounds. Horses were a common feature of street life in the 1900s; they were the traffic of the day, used for pulling buses and carriages. So being afraid of horses was the equivalent of our being afraid of cars or trucks. Even so, the intensity of Hans's fear was fairly extreme and Freud diagnosed a **phobia: an irrational fear of some object or situation**.

The psychoanalytic school of thought comes complete with suitcases full of fairly complex ideas about the *affective* aspects of 'the whole person'. It's impossible to summarise all these ideas here, but one of them is especially important for our understanding of Hans's case. Freud argues that the troublesome anxieties and neuroses we experience as adults originate in our childhood experiences and interactions. So, for example, if you are excessively mean or stubborn or addicted as an adult, this may be a kind of delayed reaction to some relationship or event you experienced as a child. And since phobias are a kind of neurosis, psychoanalysts argue that these 'irrational fear reactions' can be explained by talking about our earliest memories and interactions. Of course, adults often find this process of sifting through the past difficult and painful. For Hans, though, it was relatively easy since he didn't have to go so far back.

Freud met and corresponded with Hans's father regularly. Together they examined the boy's statements and reactions to various domestic situations, always looking for clues that might lead to an explanation for his fear of horses. Freud maintained that if he could find the origin of Hans's phobia, he could then set about treating its symptoms. Here's what he came up with:

> ### Why Hans was scared of horses: a psychoanalytic explanation
> Hans was competing with this father for the affection of his mother. As a result of this rivalry Hans was frightened of what his father would do to him. He was so small and weak and his father was so big and strong and he was scared that his father would attack him and punish him by chopping his penis off. But because expressing feelings of fear and hatred towards his father was socially and domestically unacceptable, Hans unconsciously displaced his feelings onto horses, who had a great many of the characteristics his father had. They were big and strong, they had whiskers and wore glasses (blinkers). So Hans was using horses as a scapegoat for his fear towards his father.

A fascinating explanation. *But is it right?* Well, it depends who you talk to. It has plenty of supporters, especially from within the psychoanalytic school of thought. Remember, that's the one that sees psychology as the study of the *affective* aspects of 'the whole person' and that sees our behaviour as being influenced by *unconscious* motives. If you talk to psychologists who use this *paradigm* you'll find a lot of them will regard Freud's explanation of Hans's phobia as being *right*.

But if you talk to people from other schools of thought you'll get a different response. If you talk to behaviourists you'll find they'll tend to regard Freud's interpretation as wide of the mark. And if you talk to enough of them you'll probably find one or two who'll replace Freud's explanation with their own, alternative explanation for Hans's phobia, one that fits more closely with their own school of thought or *paradigm*. Here's an example:

> ### Why Hans was scared of horses: a behaviourist explanation
> Hans exhibited a fear response whenever he came in contact with horses, horse-drawn vehicles or any object associated with horses, like muzzles and bridles. His response goes back to an incident he witnessed where a horse-drawn van collapsed in the street. This frightened him at the time and thereafter he generalised his fear

response from that particular horse-drawn vehicle to all such vehicles, all horses and all horse accessories.

This explanation is less complex than Freud's. It was put forward by Wolpe and Rachman in 1960. They see phobias as *fear responses* that are associated with particular *phobic objects*. In Hans's case the *phobic object* was horses and he generalised his *fear response* to anything connected with horses – carts, bridles, muzzles and so on. Notice that Wolpe and Rachman don't mention *emotions* or *unconscious motives* in their explanation. This is because they are using a behaviourist *paradigm*, which means that they concentrate on observable actions and responses rather than inner feelings and motives.

So is Wolpe and Rachman's explanation right? Other behaviourists may well think that it is. Psychoanalysts, though, would be unlikely to. In other words, it depends who you talk to.

Freud's research into the case of Little Hans was carried out using a psychoanalytic *paradigm*. Many other researchers from the psychoanalytic school of thought agree with his explanations of Hans's phobia, whilst behaviourists (and cognitive psychologists) are more likely to disagree with him. Some behaviourists, like Wolpe and Rachman, have even replaced Freud's conclusions with conclusions of their own. This illustrates one of those rare circumstances under which psychologists are prepared to use this troublesome 'r-word'. They may regard conclusions drawn from research data as *right* if they share the *paradigm* of whoever carried out the research.

The word *right* is a hot potato in psychology. Ask your tutor if a theory or a conclusion is *right* and she'll surely squirm a little. In this section I've tried to explain why she reacts as she does. *Right* is a word that's rarely used by psychologists, probably because there are so many contradictory and competing theories about every aspect of human behaviour.

But there are some circumstances under which psychologists may be tempted to say that something is right. One is when they're talking about testable hypotheses. Another is when they're talking about research that is carried out by someone who shares their paradigm.

▶ **The last word**

This introduction to the language of psychology should save you a lot of trouble and embarrassment. Perhaps now you'll think twice before claiming that you've 'proved Milgram's theory of obedience' or that 'excessive breast feeding causes heavy smoking in later life' or that 'cognitive dissonance theory is right'.

Although 'prove' and 'cause' and 'right' are old words that are in common use, be aware that they have new meanings in psychology. So when you're within earshot of your tutors, lecturers and examiners, think three times about how you use them.

Before you turn away from this chapter, check you've got a grasp of these new words and concepts. They all figure somewhere in Chapter 1:

- the Scientific Method
- paradigm
- empiricism
- theory
- hypothesis
- ecological validity

2 Skills for Writing Psychology Essays

Whether you're facing end-of-year examinations or modular assignments, it's likely that a hefty proportion of the assessment for your course will involve writing essays. In this chapter we'll look at some typical psychology essay questions and some devices to help you answer them.

Essay writing is undoubtedly an art in itself. Plenty of students never learn the art and are left in possession of knowledge and understanding but without the means to express their ideas on paper. This chapter is designed to reduce the number of psychology students who fit this description.

Who thinks up psychology essay questions? Teachers, lecturers, examiners. They may be from different backgrounds and have different tastes and personalities but when it comes to thinking up psychology essay questions they all think along similar lines, since the questions they come up with all fall into the same two distinct types.

Before we look at these two distinct types it's worth stopping for a moment to consider what your tutor, lecturer or examiner is interested in when she sets you a question on, for example, the psychology of *health promotion*. She's not just trying to find out how much you know about health promotion, she's also trying to find out how much you know about writing psychology essays. She wants to assess how well you know the topic *and* how well you express your ideas on paper. She wants to assess both your *knowledge* of health promotion and your *skills for writing psychology essays*. It's these *skills for writing psychology essays* that are the focus of this chapter.

So what about these two different types of essay question?

Whether you're facing end-of-year examinations or modular assignments you'll find the questions come in two distinct flavours: '**structured essays**' and '**all in ones**'. Some students prefer one type, some prefer the other. Some examples of each type will help you understand more about the distinction.

    A typical **structured essay**:
        (a) Describe psychological research into health promotion.   (*8 marks*)
        (b) Evaluate this research.   (*10 marks*)
        (c) Using your knowledge of health promotion, suggest a programme that would encourage children to eat more healthily.   (*6 marks*)

   A typical **all in one**:
   Describe and evaluate psychological research into human altruism and bystander intervention.   (*24 marks*)

So what's the difference?

Typical *structured essays* have two characteristics. First, they require you to complete separate tasks for each separate part of the question. In our example on health promotion *part (a)* requires you to **describe** research, whilst *part (b)* requires you to **evaluate** research. As we'll discover later in this chapter, these separate, distinct tasks require you to have quite separate, distinct skills. The second characteristic of *structured essays* is that you're told how many marks are available for each part of the question. This helps you to decide how much time and space to devote to each part. For example, you should devote a quarter of your time and space to *part (c)* of the question on health promotion, since it's worth a quarter of the overall mark (6 out of 24).

   Structured essays appeal to a lot of students because of the extra guidance they offer and because they reduce the need for planning and organising, since much of this is done for you.

   All in one essays tend to appeal to students who like more freedom to develop their arguments in their own way. They like to plan their answers themselves without the restrictions of the *a, b, c* format. Being someone who likes to be told what to do, I prefer *structured essays*. But that's just a personal preference.

The point is that whichever type of essay question your tutor, lecturer or examiner presents you with, you'll need a cartload of *skills for writing psychology essays* if you're going to provide a quality answer. An extensive *knowledge* of the topic you're being asked about won't be enough. You'll need to demonstrate the *skills* necessary for expressing your *knowledge* in a lively, well-informed, coherent psychology essay. The rest of this chapter deals with these necessary *skills*.

▶ Skill no. 1: Reading the words in the question

It's been said that psychology essay questions are written in code. What people mean when they say this is that *certain words* in these questions have special meanings for psychology students, tutors, lecturers and examiners, so they can't just be taken at face value. They have to be *read in a certain way*. Or, if you prefer, decoded. Studying psychology enables you to learn how to *read these words in a certain way* and so to understand what the essay questions are asking you to do.

There are two types of words in essay questions that need to be decoded. Firstly there are **the psychology words**. These are the **words that tell you what your essay should be about**. They are technical and psychological terms that don't have a great deal of meaning outside the study of human behaviour. To understand these words you need to have a sound *knowledge* of your topic. Let's take one of our example essay questions and pick out the psychology words in it:

> Describe and evaluate psychological research into human altruism and bystander intervention.

A good way of identifying the psychology words is to show the question to someone (of reasonable intelligence) who's never studied psychology and wait for them to point at a word and say 'What does that mean?' Try this exercise with your lodger or the woman up the road. In the example we're using they'll probably point to **altruism** and **bystander intervention**. These are the psychology words. Outside of psychology, their meaning is not well known.

So what do you do with them when you've identified them?

When you're writing your essay a good way of getting started is to first *identify* and then *define* (or, if you prefer, decode) the technical and psychological terms in the question. Beginning your essay with clear, concise *definitions* of the psychology words immediately puts your reader in the picture; it's a neat way of demonstrating your *knowledge* of the topic and, importantly, it gets you off the starting blocks. So a possible opening sentence would be:

> Altruism, sometimes called 'pro-social behaviour' means behaviour that is unselfish, performed for the sake of someone else, without any personal gain . . .

Earlier I said there are *two* types of words in essay questions that you need to be on the look out for. The second type are **the instructions**. Once you've defined the psychology words in the question, you need to know **what you're going to *do* in your essay**. How will you *use* your knowledge of *altruism* and *bystander intervention*? This is where the instructions come in.

Unlike the psychology words, the instructions are everyday words with everyday meanings. But when they appear in psychology essay questions they also have other, more precise, specialised meanings which are well understood by tutors, lecturers and examiners. Code meanings, if you like. If you're to produce a quality answer to the question you, too, need to learn these specialised meanings. You need to be able to *read these words in a certain way*. Sounds like hard work, I know. But the good news is there are only ten or so of these instruction words – an all-time *Top Ten* of classic instructions that crop up again and again in essay questions.

Box 2A defines and decodes them for you. Unlike most *Top Tens*, there aren't hundreds of other instruction words being released every week and straining to break into the chart. We've had the same *Top Ten* for the last 20 years.

As Box 2A shows, these words are all in common everyday use. But you need to read them in a more precise, specialised manner for the purpose of writing psychology essays. Let's take a look at the instructions in one of our example questions:

> (a)   Describe psychological research into health promotion.
> *(8 marks)*

Box 2A   Top ten instructions in essay questions

In an essay question, this one's asking you to . . .
1 **Describe**   . . . provide details of some concept, theory or study, without any opinions. It's a neutral account that has no evaluations of any kind. (*An ever popular, all-time favourite, especially for the first part of a structured essay.*)
2 **Evaluate**   . . . look in detail at the positive and negative features of a concept, theory or study. You'd substantiate this with supporting and critical evidence and maybe some of your own ideas. (*This one always carries a lot of marks. Often appears as 'critically evaluate'. 'Assess' and 'critically assess' mean the same, too.* See later in this chapter for a guide to evaluating.)
3 **Apply**   . . . write about the usefulness, in a real-world setting, of a concept, theory or study. For instance, which pro- fessionals would be interested in a particular type of research finding? (*Up and coming. More and more tutors, lecturers and examiners are waking up to the real-world application of psychology.*)
4 **Discuss**   . . . provide details of some concept, theory or study, including supporting and critical arguments that are backed up with evidence and maybe some of your own opinions. More partial than impartial. You may even talk about practical, real-world uses and implications here. (*An all-time favourite. A bit old-fashioned but still very popular. Involves elements of each of the 'top three'*).
5 **Define**   . . . explain, in precise terms, what a word or phrase means. (*A classic. Often used as a starter in structured essays.*)
6 **Explain**   . . . take a concept, theory, study and make it easy for the reader to understand. Give reasons for the exis- tence or development of the concept, theory or study, so that the reader understands how it came about.

Box 2A *continued*

	(*Tricky, due to its vagueness. Includes elements of* description, *plus a requirement to trace the* origin *of a concept. On its way down the chart, although still pretty common.*)
7 **Outline**	. . . run through the most important aspects of a concept, theory or study, leaving out the fine details. (*The skill here is to select the important points and leave out the unnecessary detail. More difficult than it looks.*)
8 **Compare**	. . . look at two or more concepts, theories or studies in relation to each other. This involves bringing out their relative good and bad points. So it's a critical, as well as descriptive, exercise. (*Less popular these days, though still around. Often appears alongside* 'contrast', *inviting you to bring out similarities* and *differences between two concepts, theories, studies.*)
9 **Illustrate**	. . . explain the meaning of a concept, word or phrase, citing examples or even diagrams to support and clarify your explanation. (*This is like* defining, *plus examples*).
10 **Analyse**	. . . take a close-up, detailed look at some concept, theory or study. This may involve dividing something up and examining each of its parts separately. (*Includes elements of* evaluation, *since you'll be looking at the merits and drawbacks of whatever is under your scrutiny.* 'Examine' *and* 'critically examine' *mean more or less the same thing.*)

   (b) Evaluate this research. (*10 marks*)

   (c) Using your knowledge of health promotion, suggest a programme that would encourage children to eat more healthily. (*6 marks*)

Clearly, this essay is going to be about **health promotion**. These are the psychology words in the question. In 1984 The World Health Organisation defined **health promotion** as:

The process of enabling people to increase control over, and to improve, their health habits.

Defining the psychological, technical terms in the question like this is an effective way of beginning your essay. It demonstrates to your reader, right from the outset, that you know your topic.

But what about the instructions? How are you going to use your knowledge of health promotion?

All right, I'm coming to that.

In their research into *health promotion* psychologists have learned a number of things about how health professionals have attempted to encourage people to behave in ways that maintain good health and to avoid behaviours that lead to ill health. In *part (a)* of your essay you'll need to *describe* some examples of this research. You should adopt a *neutral, non-evaluative* style, whilst looking in detail at the *aims* of the research, *how it was carried out* and what the *findings* were. Here's an example of a pretty good *description* of Meyerowitz and Chaiken's 1987 study into *health promotion*:

> in which the researchers wanted to find out about the effect of health education messages on breast self-examination. They divided their participants into two conditions, A and B. Condition A were given messages that emphasised the positive benefits of self-examination, whilst Condition B were given messages that emphasised the negative outcomes of non-examination. It was found that both messages increased the likelihood of and intention to examine in the short term. But in the long term (four months after the messages) Condition A were more likely to carry out regular examinations. These results suggest that positive health education messages are more effective in the long term than negative, fear-arousing, messages.

In *part (b)* of your essay you'll move on to look in detail at the positive and negative features of the research into *health promotion*. You'll probably deal with many of the same studies and theories you *described* in *part (a)*. See *skill 4* later in this chapter for a guide to evaluating studies and theories.

Although *part (c)* doesn't feature any of our *top ten instructions*, you're clearly being invited to write about the usefulness, in a real-world setting, of the research into *health promotion*. So *part (c)* is about *applying* studies and theories (number 3 in our *top ten*) (*skill 4*, later in this chapter, has some more on applying psychological evidence).

Reading the words in the question: the main points again

- When you're presented with a psychology essay question look out for **the psychology words** and **the instructions**.
- **The psychology words** tell you what the subject matter of the essay is. These relate to your *knowledge* of psychology.
- Begin your essay by defining **the psychology words**.
- **The instructions** tell you what to do with your knowledge.
- The *top ten* **instructions** tend to crop up over and over again in psychology essay questions. Make sure you learn their precise, specialised meanings.

▶ Skill no. 2: Planning

Chances are that by the time you reach the *essay planning* stage you'll either be sitting in your room poised to write one of your modular assignments or you'll be in a gymnasium somewhere sitting an end-of-term examination. Whichever category you're in you'll either be staring at a *structured essay* question or you'll be looking down the barrel of an *all in one*. The *knowledge* you need for writing your essay will either be at your fingertips (if you're writing a modular assignment) or in your memory store (if you're in the gym) and you'll have thoroughly *read and decoded* the words in the question. All you need to do now is get started on that first paragraph.

But wait. You can't simply start writing. Not just like that. There are some things you need to sort out first, some questions you need to ask yourself. Like, for example:

1 How much time do I have?
2 What's my word limit?
3 What shall I include?
4 What shall I leave out?
5 What order shall I present my material in?

These are the questions that a carefully thought-out, clearly presented **essay plan** should answer for you. If you begin your essay without considering them it's unlikely you'll make the most of your knowledge. You'll probably find yourself running out of time, including irrelevant material, answering the wrong question or coming up against a number of other common difficulties. So let's look at each of these questions in turn.

1. How much time do I have? This is a question you'll ask yourself when you're working in the gym, under time-constrained conditions. Psychology exam essay questions usually allow 45 or 60 minutes. Spend **the first five minutes** working on your **essay plan**. If you're working on a **structured essay** be sure to take note of how many marks are up for grabs for each part of the question and allocate your time accordingly. Also, if you finish early, although it's tempting to sit and look at the rope ladders, resist. Use the spare time to proof-read your essays. You'll almost certainly be able to claw in a few extra marks.

2. What's my word limit? This is a question you'll ask yourself if you're working on a modular assignment. These essays tend to have 1000, 1500 or 2000 words limits. Your **essay plan** should ensure that you fulfil all the requirements of the question, at the appropriate level of detail, without overstepping the word-count. Sounds like a tall order. So spend **an hour or so** devising and revising your **essay plan** *before* you begin your first paragraph. If you're working on a **structured essay** check the number of marks allocated for each part of the question and divide up your words accordingly. Finally, don't *understep* the word limit. If you think you've answered the question and you've still got 300 words to play with, you've included too little detail.

3. What shall I include? Anyone planning any kind of psychology essay will ask themselves this question. The answer is **include concepts, studies and theories that relate directly to the *psychology words* and *the instructions* that are featured in the question**. So if it relates to the appropriate *topic* and the appropriate *skills*, you can put it in. A clear plan of *what* material you're going to include and *how* you're going to use it will enable you to *stick to the question* as you're answering it. Never let it out of your sight.

4. What shall I leave out? Ruthlessness, a quality normally associated with fat cats, central defenders and park-keepers, is a quality *you'll* need when you're answering this question. A lot of well-prepared psychology students try to include *all* their knowledge of the topic in their essays, even though it means *misreading* the psychology words *and* the instructions in the question. For example, when answering a social psychology question about *'the dissolution of relationships'* a student might include concepts, studies and theories relating to *'the formation and dissolution of relationships'*. If you ask them why, they might say 'because it's what I revised' or 'because it was all one topic when we did it in class'. Use your **essay plan** to help you ensure that you **leave out superfluous material**. Including it wastes times and doesn't gain you any marks. Be ruthless.

5. What order shall I present my material in? Your **essay plan** should provide you with a carefully thought-out, clearly presented, fingertip guide to what to include in your essay. It should also tell you what *order* to present your material in. The most common way of ordering your material is to use a *linear* approach, where you simply make a list of 'things to include', starting at the top with the *introduction* and finishing at the bottom with the *conclusion*. Although this *linear* approach is widely used and pretty effective, I'm going to suggest an alternative. Instead of *lists*, I'm going to suggest *patterns*.

In his book *Use Your Head* (1995) Tony Buzan observes that when most people plan speeches, seminars, meetings and essays they tend to use a linear framework: they make lists. The problem with this method (Buzan suggests) is that it doesn't fit in with the way we *think*. When we use our heads to plan and solve problems, rather than organising our ideas into lists we organise them into *patterns*. These patterns take the form of lots of ideas that are *connected* to lots of other ideas in the pattern. This means that when one of these ideas pops into our head it can spark off a *connection* with any one of a number of other ideas.

This view of thinking differs from the traditional, *linear* view of the way we plan and solve problems, where one idea inevitably leads on to the next idea, which inevitably leads on to the next and so on. For Buzan our thought processes take the form of **patterns of ideas with**

interrelated connections, rather than lists of ideas with linear connections. And because we *think* in patterns, Buzan says that we should plan our seminars, meetings, speeches and essays in the same way. So instead of *linear plans* for essays we should make **patterned plans** for essays.

*How do you make a **patterned plan**?*

Let's say you're working on this essay question: *Describe and evaluate psychological research into the dissolution of relationships.*

To make a **patterned plan** for this essay, find yourself a blank sheet of paper. In the centre of it write down what the essay is going to be about. This will be your **central idea**. For this essay you could use *'the dissolution of relationships'* You could say these are **the psychology words**, though they're not especially 'technical'. Even so, social psychologists would certainly regard them as 'psychological terms'.

Next, write the names of the concepts, theories and studies you want to include in your essay around the outside of your **central idea**. We'll call these your **related ideas**. Now draw some lines connecting the **central idea** to the **related ideas** and then from each **related idea** draw some more lines that point to some extra information about various aspects of these **related ideas**. Such aspects would include *descriptions* and *evaluations* of the concepts, studies and theories you're dealing with. This anchors your **plan** firmly to **the instructions** in the question.

Now you've got a **plan** showing details of all the ideas you're going to include in your essay. Next you can decide what *order* you want to present these ideas in. Do this by numbering your **related ideas** according to the order you want them to appear in.

Some students who use this method embellish their **Plan** with colours, pictures, symbols etc. This is fine, so long as you're not working under time-constrained conditions. **Box 2B** shows the typical shape of a **patterned plan**. Notice its swirly, personalised style. This owes much to the fact that it's meant to reflect the 'shape' of its author's thought processes.

There's no doubt that using a *linear plan* for essays can be effective and is certainly preferable to having no plan at all. But arguably **patterned plans** have several advantages over the *linear* version. They enable you to represent connections and *links* between different con-

Box 2B   Patterned plans tend to have an idiosyncratic, personalised style

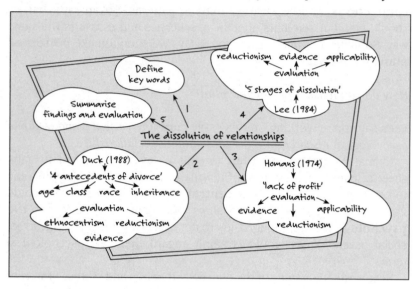

cepts, theories and studies in your essay. They give you extra *space* and flexibility so that you can introduce new ideas into your plan whenever they occur to you. Also, they make it easier for you to delay your decision about putting your material in *order* until you've got all your ideas down on paper.

Planning: the main points again

*   In an exam spend *the first five minutes* on each essay working on your *essay plan.*
*   For a modular assignment spend *an hour or so* working on your *essay plan.*
*   Include concepts, studies and theories that relate directly to **the psychology words** and **the instructions** that are featured in the essay question.
*   Irrelevant material wastes time and gains no marks.
*   Any *essay plan* is better than no plan at all, but *patterned plans* can be especially effective.

▶ Skill no. 3: Writing with style

People who mark psychology essays don't have it easy. Tutors, lecturers and examiners routinely mark 60 or 70 essays at a sitting and, apart from a few fanatics, they'd really rather be doing something else. So spare them a thought. Remember you have it within your power to make their work more enjoyable. An essay that's written coherently, purposefully, in a *style that considers the needs of the reader* will be more effective than one that has just as much psychological content but which the reader has to fight tooth and nail to fathom.

So as you begin your first paragraph, consider this maxim: **a happy reader makes a generous marker**. Here are a handful of hints on how to write psychology essays in a *style that considers the needs of the reader.*

Write for the novice

When you write a postcard home from a holiday you've got a clear picture of who's going to read it. You don't just *write* a postcard, you write it *to* somebody. The same applies when you write a psychology essay. Think for a moment about the kind of person who'll be reading your work. Your tutor, lecturer or examiner will probably be of above-average intelligence, they'll have a good command of written language and they'll be an expert in psychology. It's this third trait (characteristic) that often gets in the way of a good essay, **because as a psychology student you're required to disregard it**.

Students who write their essays for the *intelligent, literate* **expert** encounter difficulties because they should really be writing for someone who only has the first two of these traits. That is, an *intelligent, literate* **novice**. The sad thing is that on many psychology courses this convention is never properly pointed out. Tutors often wait for it to *dawn* on their students, which, in many cases, never happens. So let's have it out in the open:

> Your reader needs to have all psychological and technical terms that don't have a great deal of meaning outside the study of human behaviour (what we've been calling **the psychology words**) defined and clarified for them as they're introduced into your essay.

Don't just mention them and move on. Say what they mean. For example, in an essay dealing with Freud's 1909 case study of Little Hans (for a full outline of this study see Chapter 1) you might write something like:

> Freud argued that Hans's irrational fear of horses masked an underlying fear of his father, which had been driven into his **unconscious** by a process of **repression**. Freud regarded the unconscious as a vast store of unpleasant, often socially unacceptable fears, memories and desires that are held out of reach of our conscious thoughts. Repression is a Freudian term that refers to the process of pushing these unpleasant ideas into the unconscious . . .

Here **the psychology words** (in bold type) are defined and clarified *as they're introduced*. Notice how this excerpt is written with an *intelligent, literate novice* in mind. It's clearly meant for someone who isn't familiar with Freud's theory. If it were written for an *intelligent, literate expert* the first sentence would be enough on its own.

The reason you're required to *write for the novice* in psychology essays is so you can demonstrate your knowledge of the subject. Students who *write for the expert* (and plenty do) lose the chance to pick up marks because they assume too much knowledge on the part of their reader. This is a bit like writing a postcard home and not mentioning the weather, assuming everyone already knows it's raining.

What paragraphs are for

A student I know did a little experiment. He handed in copies of one of his psychology essays to two different tutors. Each tutor received the same essay except that *tutor A's* copy had no paragraphs: it was written in uninterrupted dense text. Predictably enough, *tutor B*, who received the essay with the paragraphs left in, reported significantly higher feelings of satisfaction after reading the essay *and* awarded a significantly higher grade. It might have been that *tutor A* was a meaner marker and this contributed to what happened here. But it's also likely that **writing with paragraphs increases the effectiveness of essays**.

So what do paragraphs do?

Well, they ease the job of the reader by providing a **separation between ideas, or aspects of ideas**. And for a bog-eyed tutor, lecturer or examiner who's already read 50 essays before breakfast, writing that is separated into ideas (and aspects of ideas) is a breath of fresh air.

You should use paragraphs to parcel off what you write into sections. For example, if an essay question asks you to 'Outline psychological research into phobias' you'd probably want to write about a number of studies, so you'd devote a separate paragraph to each separate study. Alternatively, if a question asked you to 'Discuss Freud's case study of Little Hans' (see Chapter 1 for a discussion of this case) you'd be required to look at this study in quite a lot of detail, so you'd devote separate paragraphs to separate *aspects* of the study. The general rule is **each new idea deserves a new paragraph**. For example, I'm going to start another one now.

A final word about paragraphs. **Links.** These are what you use to move from one paragraph to another. In the interests of keeping the reader satisfied and attentive, keep your links *smooth*. Avoid sudden changes of tack as they can destroy the continuity of your writing. Here's an example of a *smooth link* between two paragraphs from an essay about the case of Little Hans:

> On the whole a great many behaviourists have been critical of Freud's work because of his use of the concept of the unconscious mind, which, behaviourists argue, is unobservable and therefore difficult for psychologists to study empirically . . .
>
> **Another school who have criticised Freud** are cognitive psychologists, who denounce his emphasis on the emotional life of the humans. They say he neglects our thinking and problem solving capacities . . .

Notice how the *linking* phrase (in bold) eases the transition between the two ideas being discussed. This is good for continuity and good for the satisfaction level of the reader.

Words to avoid whenever possible

In Chapter 1 I tried to explain why psychologists are so wary about using words like *proof, cause* and *right* when they talk and write about the study of human behaviour. These are just three of a select group of words that should either be used *with extreme caution*, or *avoided altogether* when writing psychology essays. These are words that perplex psychology tutors, lecturers and examiners because of their vagueness, inaccuracy or their lack of an agreed definition. **Box 2C**

Box 2C Top ten words to avoid whenever possible

Whenever possible, avoid using these words in essays . . .	
1 **Prove**	. . . because, as Chapter 1 indicates, psychologists generally accept that their theories cannot be proven, merely supported by evidence gained from testing hypotheses. Replace with **support**.
2 **Cause**	. . . because whilst we can often observe a consistent relationship between two variables, we needn't assume one is causing the other. Extraneous variables often interfere with causal conclusions. This word can sometimes be replaced with **correlates with**. See Chapter 1 for a full explanation.
3 **Right**	. . . unless you're referring to directly testable hypotheses. Theories (and statements taken from them), however, cannot be shown to be 'right' because they're not directly testable. Replace with **supported**. Chapter 1 explains more fully.
4 **Believe**	. . . when writing about researchers' conclusions and theories because you're referring not to 'beliefs' but to states of mind arrived at in the light of research. So avoid writing 'Festinger believes'. It sounds too much like idle speculation. Replace with **argues**, **concludes**, **states**, **suggests**.
5 **Man**	. . . when you really mean 'human'. Avoid phrases like 'man's achievements' and 'man's history'. Replace with **human**.
6 **Tribe**	. . . when writing about cross-cultural research. Most social scientists regard this as an outmoded and imprecise word these days. Avoid writing 'Aboriginal tribes'. Replace with **culture** or **community** or **group**.

Box 2C *continued*

7	**Animals**	. . . when writing about psychological research that relates to species other than humans. Terms like 'research on animals' comes across as vague, since distinctions between humans and animals are hotly disputed. Replace with **non-humans**.
8	**Subconscious**	. . . when writing about Freudian psychoanalysis. This word is often (mistakenly) used by students when they mean 'unconscious' or 'pre-conscious', both of which are Freudian terms. Subconscious isn't. Replace with **unconscious** or **pre-conscious**, depending on which you mean.
9	**Mental**	. . . when writing about abnormal psychology. Terms like 'mental problems', 'mental institutions' are to be avoided. This is an imprecise, outmoded word in abnormal psychology, though for cognitive psychologists it has a more modern feel. Goodish replacements are **psychological** or **psychiatric**.
10	**Subject**	. . . when referring to those who are being studied in psychological research. It gives the impression of passive subservience. Whilst this may be close to the truth in some cases, most social scientists now prefer to use the word **participant**.

has my *top ten* words to avoid whenever possible, plus some possible replacements.

Some of these words are just plain old-fashioned. It may be that eventually some of the replacements I've suggested will suffer the same fate. It's in the nature of psychology to have a 'transient terminology' that discards and replaces words as it goes along. In the meantime (perhaps for the next ten years or so) a policy of avoiding anything in the *top ten* is a good one.

Your ideas and other people's ideas

'*Can I use my own opinions in my essay?*' is one of the *top ten most common questions* students ask their tutors before they write psychology essays. And it's a hard one to answer. On the one hand, tutors don't want to encourage students to write essays that are overloaded with polemic and personal prejudice. On the other hand, they don't want to be accused of clamping down on original thought. Consequently the question is often left dangling.

'*Well can I or can't I?*' The answer goes something like this: '*Yes but and Yes but*'. Two yesses, both with conditions attached to them:

- The first **Yes but** . . . your opinions will be much more effective where they're supported with psychological evidence, that is, concepts, studies and theories that back them up. In this respect, your opinions are just as valid as anyone else's. If you include Freud's opinions, Piaget's opinions or Milgram's opinions without any psychological evidence to support them your essay won't be especially effective. So yes, by all means include your opinions, but back them up with concepts, studies and theories from psychology wherever possible.

- The second **Yes but** . . . opinions that aren't supported by psychological evidence should only be used sparingly, for example, as a supplement to other ideas that are presented in the light of research. It may be that you come up with an opinion or idea that hasn't been widely researched by psychologists, or one that no one else has thought of. In cases like this it's fine to include your opinion in your essay but don't overload your essay with this type of unsupported, anecdotal opinion. If unsupported opinions are used sparingly and they're relevant to the question, include them.

Here are two examples of personal opinions that have been used effectively in an essay. Both excerpts have been lifted out of an answer to *Part (C)* of a *structured essay* on *the psychology of stress*, where you're asked to 'Describe ways in which a person may prepare in advance for stressful events':

Example 1
One way of preparing in advance for a stressful event (like a job interview or a driving test) would be to talk to friends and family about your apprehensions and anxieties. Social support networks can lighten stressful feelings associated with forthcoming events. Folkman et al. (1986) support this idea with a theory which sets out a variety of strategies for coping with stress. One of the strate-

gies they recognise is 'seeking social support', involving asking for advice, talking to friends and family. In their study they . . .

Example 2
Another way of reducing the stressful effects of a forthcoming event would be to attend a course in meditation and breath control at a local Buddhist Centre for the weeks leading up to the event. Developing ways of regulating, attending to and controlling our breathing can enhance our powers of coping . . .

Note how, in *example 1* the opinion is supported and made more convincing by the use of evidence from psychological research. Using personal opinion in this way is the most advisable and effective method. But *example 2* is a perfectly legitimate use of a personal opinion, since it does relate directly the question. It's a valid suggestion too, which, to be fair, needs to be researched. Be careful, though – too much of this type of *unsupported* opinion doesn't go down well.

Here are two final thoughts on *your ideas and other people's ideas.*

Firstly, the '**I think**' problem. Look again at the two examples from the essay on *stress* and you'll notice that even though personal opinions have been included, the student has refrained from using the term 'I think'. Whether to encourage students to write 'I think' in their essays is something that different tutors, lecturers and examiners have different ideas about. Some say it sounds too informal, too homespun. Some say it's a good way of encouraging students to have original ideas. Because of this internal division amongst psychologists, it's probably best to avoid it. Look at it this way: if you include an idea that isn't credited to anyone else, it's fairly clear that it's yours.

Secondly, when you use *other people's ideas* in your essay you need to **give credit where it's due** – to the original authors. There are three ways of doing this: **quoting**, **citing** and **referencing**.

Quoting other psychologists in essays, especially at length, isn't popular with tutors, lecturers or examiners. If you do think it necessary to include the odd quote here and there, follow it with the *author's name* and *date* of the publication the quote comes from. Most markers also prefer you to give the *page number* of the book where the quote appears.

Citing is necessary when you refer to any piece of psychological evidence in your essay. *Cite* the author and *give the date* of publication of the research. There's an example of this in *example 1* above. The date of publication gives the reader a clearer, more historical picture of developments in psychology. If the research you're citing was carried out by *a pair* of researchers, include both names. If it's an *entourage*, you can use *et al.* like the student in *example 1* has.

Referencing is necessary when you've written a modular assignment. It isn't expected in exams. Include a reference section at the end of your essay, listing all the books you've used. There are strict conventions for *referencing* so be sure to go along with them. If you're referencing a book it's: *author's name, (date), title, city of publication, publisher.* If you're referencing a paper from a journal it's: *author's name, (date), title of paper, title of journal, volume, page numbers.* So, for one of the books I've been using, the reference would be: T. Buzan (1995), *Use Your Head*, London, BBC Books. For more examples of referencing look in the reference section of this book.

Ending

There's an art to ending an essay. My final thought on *writing with style* is to ask you to consider the needs of your reader one last time. Leave them with a pleasant aftertaste. End your essay smoothly, not abruptly. Bring things to a close thoughtfully, seamlessly, perhaps by summarising some of the points you've made, perhaps by reiterating an overall conclusion of some sort, perhaps by suggesting some ideas for future research. But whatever you do, don't just stop. Some endings come so suddenly that the reader is left with the idea that the writer has been called away unexpectedly. So when you've finished, reread your final sentence and ask yourself if it reads like a carefully thought-out ending or like a sudden

---

Writing with style: the main points again

- Pitch your essay at the level of the intelligent, literate **novice**.
- Writing with **paragraphs** increases the effectiveness of essays.
- Steer clear of using any of the **'top ten words to avoid' whenever possible**.
- Use your own opinions in your essays where they're supported by evidence. If you use unsupported opinions, do it sparingly and relevantly.
- When you use other people's ideas **give credit where it's due** by quoting, citing and referencing.
- Bring your essay to a thoughtful close.

▷ Skill no. 4: Evaluating studies and theories

If you read the instructions in any psychology essay question, it's obvious that your chances of producing a quality answer without a heavy dose of *evaluating studies and theories* are slim. Look again at our *Top Ten instructions* (in Box 2A) and notice how many of them have the skill of *evaluating* right at their core. *Evaluating, applying, discussing, comparing* and *analysing* psychological evidence all involve writing about the positive and negative aspects of studies and theories. And it's almost unheard of for tutors, lecturers or examiners to set essays that don't have any of these words, or their close relatives, in them.

In the pecking order of *skills for writing psychology essays*, **evaluating studies and theories** is at the front of the queue. True, *describing* research and *applying* it to real-life situations are important, but this 'e-word' is where the big prizes are. So let's work out *how to evaluate studies and theories.* Better still, let's develop *a system for evaluating studies and theories.* And let's call it **the DRREEEEEAAAMSS system**.

The first thing you need to consider when you're *evaluating* evidence is that you should be writing about **positive** *and* **negative** aspects of studies and theories. *Evaluating* isn't just *criticising*. It involves being *complimentary* as well as critical.

But what about these DRREEEEEAAAMSS?

I'm coming to that.

The second thing you need to consider is what *criteria* you're going to use to evaluate psychological evidence. And this is where **the DRREEEEEAAAMSS system** comes in. There's a long list of *evaluation criteria* you can use to highlight the positive and negative aspects of psychological evidence. As you're *planning* and *writing* your essay you need to be sure to refer to *as many of these criteria as you can* for each study and theory you include. You can use **the DRREEEEEAAAMSS system** as a checklist to ensure you don't short-change your reader by leaving out relevant *evaluation criteria*.

So DRREEEEEAAAMSS basically refers to a list of things to consider when you're doing your evaluations, does it?

Correct. And it's summarised in **Box 2D**.

Hang on. This looks complicated. Am I supposed to remember all 14 of these big words?

Box 2D The DRREEEEEAAAMSS system for evaluating psychological evidence

---

DRREEEEEAAAMSS gives you 14 criteria for evaluating studies and theories.

For each **study** you evaluate use as many of the **14 criteria** as you can.

For each **theory** you evaluate use as many of the **7 asterisked criteria** as you can.

Design (the control of extraneous variables)

Replicability (whether or not a study can be repeated with the same results)

Reductionism* (explaining complex wholes in terms of their component parts)

Ethics (whether participants are harmed or deceived during research)

Ethnocentrism* (the view that one's own cultural world view is central)

Ecological validity (whether or not the research situation is true to life)

Extrapolation (whether data from non-human participants help us understand humans)

Evidence* (whether researchers' conclusions are supported by other researchers' work)

Approach* (whether evidence can be evaluated in terms of the paradigm it arises from)

Applicability* (whether or not the evidence can be put to any use in the real world)

Androcentrism* (whether or not the evidence is written from a masculine standpoint)

Method (evaluating evidence in terms of the methods that were used to gather it)

Sample (whether the participants who took part in the study were representative)

Socio-political impact* (can the evidence be used to affect situations of exploitation and oppression)

Remember that evaluation isn't just criticism. Be complimentary as well as critical.

Don't panic. When you're writing your essay you're not expected to comment on *all* 14 criteria for *every* study you evaluate. Nor are you expected to comment on *all* 7 criteria for *every* theory you include. Instead, **use the DRREEEEEAAAMSS system to help you remember the criteria and then for each study or theory you evaluate select the criteria you think are most relevant for you to comment on.** So you might end up using a handful of criteria (or more, or less) for each *study* you include, or perhaps four criteria (or more, or less) for each *theory* you include.

Spelling 'dreams' with two r's, five e's and three a's gives you a convenient way of remembering the **14 criteria for evaluating studies**. *DRREEEEEAAAMSS* is a good mnemonic (convenient way of remembering) for bringing the 14 big words to mind. **But what about evaluating theories?** Evaluating *theories* requires a slightly different approach. Some of these evaluation criteria aren't really suitable for the purpose. For example, you can't comment on the *Design* or *Method* of a *theory*, since they aren't actually pieces of research. So **the DRREEEEEAAAMSS system** offers you 7 evaluation criteria that you can use for evaluating *theories as well as studies*. They're the ones with the asterisks:

> *A*pplicability, *A*pproach, *A*ndrocentrism, *E*thnocentrism, *R*eductionism, *E*vidence, *S*ocio-political impact. Now we need a mnemonic to help you remember them. How about: ***Adam And Eve Ran Absolutely Everywhere Slowly***? Alternatively, perhaps you should make up your own: Adam And Eve Ate Rhubarb Every Saturday.

Before we look at each of these 14 'big words' in detail, I should point out that this isn't an exhaustive list of evaluation criteria. You might come up with others you yourself use for commenting on the pros and cons of psychological evidence. What **DRREEEEEAAAMSS** does give you is a healthy, balanced diet of evaluation criteria. Feel free to supplement it.

So here goes. What follows is a detailed review of the *meanings* of the 14 big words in **the DRREEEEEAAAMSS System**, along with some suggestions about how to use them in psychology essays. You probably won't remember all 14 criteria after the first (or second) reading. But when you've used them for evaluating evidence in one or two essays they'll start to stick. And before too long you should see a change for the better in the structure and quality of your work.

- **Design** refers to the steps researchers take to control **extraneous variables** in their studies (see Chapter 1 for a discussion of these). If a researcher is investigating the influence of *variable A* on *variable B* s/he'll try to control or hold constant the effect of any other (extraneous) variable that might have an influence on *B*. The problem of achieving this degree of control is a problem of *design*. A good ploy for controlling extraneous variables is to divide participants into 'matched' conditions. For instance, if you're studying how background noise (*variable A*) affects participants' problem-solving abilities (*variable B*) you might want to ensure that an extraneous variable such as *intelligence* is held constant across the two conditions (high noise and low noise). To do this you could *design* your study so that participants with high and low intelligence levels are allocated equally between the high and low noise conditions. This helps you to *isolate* the proposed link between *A* and *B*.

    In an essay, in (positively) evaluating the *design* of our experiment on *the effect of overcrowding on violent behaviour in female mice* (see Chapter 1 for a full description) you might include a statement like:

    > *The researchers have taken a number of steps to control extraneous variables such as temperature, age, season and the number of mice in each condition. These variables are all held constant across the two conditions. This strengthens the proposed link between variable A, the level of crowding, and variable B, violent behaviour.*

- **Replicability** refers to whether or not a study can be repeated to produce similar findings. Two things are at stake here. *First*, whether a study can be repeated *at all*. *Second*, whether similar results emerge *if it is* repeated. Some studies can't be repeated *at all* because they're **conducted in unique situations that are hard to replicate** – earthquakes, eclipses, coronations, etc. Psychologists refer to this type of 'one-off', unrepeatable study as **opportunistic research**. Other studies *are* repeated but they produce different findings. Psychologists refer to this as unreliable research. Studies that are opportunistic or unreliable can both be said to lack replicability. They might have interesting results but if no one can go out and *replicate* or verify them they're flawed.

    In an essay, in (negatively) evaluating the *replicability* of Freud's 1909 case study of Little Hans (see Chapter 1 for a full discussion) you might include a statement like:

This would be a difficult study to replicate because of Freud's peculiar relationship with Hans's family. Before his acquaintance with Hans's case he had previously had therapeutic relations with his mother. Also, unusually, the analysis of Hans was carried out by his father, who then passed on his interpretations to Freud 'second hand'. A similar therapeutic situation would be difficult to replicate, making Freud's findings difficult to verify.

- **Reductionism*** refers to the way psychologists sometimes try to explain complex concepts (the list is endless, but some examples are *thinking, aggression, interpersonal attraction*) in simplified terms, without recognising their complexity. A typical *reductionist* ploy is to try to explain a complex concept by focusing only on the characteristics of its constituent parts, for example, trying to explain the brain's (complex) capacity for thinking in terms of nothing more than series of neurochemical processes. Although neurochemistry is involved in thinking, *alone* it doesn't do justice to the complexity of how we *figure things out*. A fuller, more rounded explanation of thinking could include a discussion of *developmental, cognitive* and *cultural* factors as well as *neurochemical* ones. Critics of *reductionism* argue that complex concepts need to be understood **holistically, recognising the influence of a variety factors**. The motto of this approach is 'the whole is greater than the sum of its individual parts'. Unlike most of the other criteria in **DRREEEEEAAMSS**, *reductionism* is usually seen as a negative feature of psychological evidence. You'd rarely *congratulate* a theorist for being *reductionist*.

  In an essay, *reductionism* can be used as a criterion for evaluating studies *or* theories. Homans's 1974 theory of *interpersonal attraction* states that we form friendships on the basis of *profit and loss*. We choose our friends after weighing up how we can benefit from them (affection, protection, status and so on) versus what they'll cost us (time, energy, money). In evaluating (negatively) Homans's *reductionism* you might include a statement like:

  Interpersonal attraction is a complex issue. Homans's theory highlights only one aspect of the formation and breakdown of friendships – the concept of profit and loss. Whilst this may shed some light on the topic, the theory is reductionist in that it fails to discuss the full array of social, cultural, sexual and emotional factors involved.

- **Ethnocentrism*** refers to the tendency to regard other cultures (and the people and institutions that make up those cultures) solely from the perspective of one's own culture. It's a form of prejudice. Like *egocentrism*, where an individual is unable to appreciate another's point of view, *ethnocentrism* is a failure to appreciate another *culture's* **viewpoint** (or **world view**, to use a phrase favoured by social anthropologists). An *ethnocentric* world view is often accompanied by the belief that the customs and products of one's own culture are superior to those of other cultures. In psychology *ethnocentrism* is especially relevant when discussing *cross-cultural* research. As with *reductionism*, it's generally seen as a *negative* characteristic of evidence.

  In an essay, as with *reductionism*, *ethnocentrism* can be used as a criterion to evaluate studies *or* theories. In 1913 Freud theorised that the Australian Aboriginal practice wherein sons-in-law and mothers-in-law avoid social contact with each other was a *sexual taboo*. He saw it as a 'defence mechanism' that prevented the opportunity for sexual relations between sons-in-law and mothers-in-law. In evaluating (negatively) this theory on the grounds of *ethnocentrism* you might include a statement like:

  > *Freud's theory of Aboriginal mother-in-law/son-in-law avoidance was developed from afar, following his therapeutic encounters in Europe. Repressed sexual desire was a major theme in Freud's own cultural setting, whilst its influence in Aboriginal society may have been less acute. Arguably then, Freud's interpretation of these 'avoidance practices' was ethnocentric. Perhaps he was judging other cultures by the standards of his own. Hence the suggestion by other authors (Radcliffe-Brown, 1931) that Aboriginal avoidance practices had social, rather than sexual, origins.*

- **Ethics** refers to the way psychologists treat (human and non-human) participants during research. At stake here are the safety and dignity of participants. It's up to the researcher to make sure both of these are preserved. Several ethical questions are posed by psychological research. Are participants protected from physical and emotional *harm*? Do they have the opportunity to *withdraw* midway through a study? Do they give *informed consent* to be studied? Are they protected from *deception*? Do they receive a thorough *debriefing* after the research? Plenty of researchers are prepared to answer 'not really' to some of these questions in the interests of finding out more about human (and non-human) behaviour. Consequently this is a particularly fruitful criterion for evaluation (Chapter 3 has a detailed guide to *treating participants ethically*).

In an essay, evaluating (negatively) the *ethics* of Milgram's 1974 obedience study (described fully in Chapter 1) you might include a statement like:

> *There are a number of ethical problems with Milgram's study. In particular, although Milgram professed not to have expected so many participants to behave so obediently, some were visibly experiencing stress as they increased the voltage level. It could be argued that participants were unnecessarily exposed to an emotionally harmful situation.*

- **Extrapolation** refers to a philosophical debate about the difference between humans and non-humans. Some theorists regard **humans as *quantitatively* more advanced than non-humans**. They think we (humans) have behavioural and mental capacities that are of the same *kind* as those of non-humans, but which are more developed. This is sometimes described as the **behavioural continuity** argument. Others regard humans as *qualitatively* different from non-humans. According to this view we're not just more advanced, we're a different *kind* of creature. Theorists who support this view see studies using non-humans as useless for telling us anything about humans, since we can't generalise (or *extrapolate*, to use the technical term) findings from non-humans to humans (Koestler, 1970). Those who favour the behavioural continuity view *do* feel that studies of monkeys and dogs and so forth tell us something about humans. *Extrapolation* is a useful criterion for evaluating studies using non-humans.

In an essay, in evaluating (negatively) our study into *the effect of overcrowding on the violent behaviour of female mice* (see Chapter 1 for a full description) you might include a statement like:

> *Even though the mice were observed to behave more violently in the crowded condition, this doesn't necessarily tell us anything about human violent behaviour. After all, it may be a mistake to extrapolate from the behaviour of such a distantly related species to the behaviour of humans.*

- **Ecological validity** refers to how true to life a study is. Where researchers put participants in unusual *settings* and ask them to perform unusual (to them) *behaviours*, research is said to lack *ecological validity*. This is a criticism often levelled at studies that take place in laboratory settings. True, laboratory research allows researchers to have a lot of control over the variables they're studying but the downside is that their participants are more likely to behave unnaturally. This is a problem since it doesn't tell us anything about their everyday behaviour. Critics of laboratory research prefer to carry out *ecologically valid* studies that take place in **real life** (**naturalistic** is the technical term) settings – streets, cafeterias, trains, etc. This way they can observe naturally occurring behaviour. Chapter 1 has a longer discussion of ecological validity.

  In an essay, in evaluating (positively) the *ecological validity* of Milgram's own replication of his 1974 obedience study (described fully in Chapter 1), where he transferred his experiment to a run-down office block, you might include a statement like:

  > *When Milgram transferred his experiment from the Yale laboratory and into an office block, the setting was more naturalistic. Although participants were still required to perform unusual behaviours, the setting was at least common-or-garden. Participants' behaviour apparently followed suit. The obedience level fell from 65 per cent to 48 per cent. This exercise demonstrates the researcher's awareness of the importance of ecological validity.*

- **Evidence*** refers to whether or not researchers can point to other evidence to support their own. Conclusions from studies and theories are taken more seriously if other researchers have come to similar conclusions from *their* work. It's a case of 'strength in numbers'.

  In an essay you can use *evidence* to evaluate studies *or* theories. In evaluating (positively) Festinger and Carlsmith's 1959 study and theory of 'cognitive dissonance' (see Chapter 1 for a full discussion) you might include a statement like:

  > *According to the theory of 'cognitive dissonance' smokers will rate tobacco as being less harmful than non-smokers will. This is because they're attempting to reduce the amount of dissonance (incompatibility) between their behaviour (smoking) and their belief (that smoking kills). A study by McMasters and Lee (1991)*

found this to be the case. Compared to equally well-informed groups of ex-smokers and non-smokers, smokers were more likely to play down the dangers of cigarettes.

• **Approach*** refers to the relationship between a piece of evidence and the paradigm (school of thought) it's associated with. As Chapter 1 discusses at some length, there are half a dozen or so *paradigms* in psychology, each one with different ideas about its *subject matter* and its *methods for carrying out research.* Some studies and theories are more closely wedded to specific schools of thought than others are. Where there's a clear relation between a piece of research and a paradigm you can evaluate the research by evaluating the paradigm it's associated with. This is like pulling the rug from beneath the researcher (where the evaluation is negative). Another useful evaluation ploy is to comment on the paradigm underlying a piece of evidence from the point of view of *another paradigm.* So you might comment on a study which has emerged out of *psychoanalysis* from a *behaviourist* viewpoint. There's an example of this technique below.

In an essay, you can use *approach* as an evaluation criterion for studies *or* theories. In evaluating (negatively) the *approach* of Erikson's 1980 theory of life-cycle development, where he presents us with a view of human personality based on Freudian psychoanalysis, you might include a statement like:

> *Erikson shows how personality matures through a number of challenges that arise at different stages of the life cycle. However, the effectiveness of his theory depends on the effectiveness of a number of Freudian concepts upon which it is built like id, ego and super-ego. These components of personality are not observable. Theorists from a behaviourist paradigm would therefore argue that Erikson's theory is flawed because it depends upon invisible concepts that can't be measured.*

• **Applicability*** refers to whether the conclusions from studies or theories are of any use to anyone. Can they help us understand any real-life situations, issues or incidents? Can they help educators, childminders, pharmacists, athletes, police, pianists and politicians (and so forth) in their work? As well as a way of evaluating evidence, it's increasingly common for essay questions, or at least *parts* of *structured essays*, to ask you to *apply* the findings of studies and theories. So it's worth getting into the habit of thinking and writing about what *use* evidence can be put to. It's also refreshing to know that (a lot of) psychologists are providing society with a service.

In an essay, *applicability* can be used to evaluate studies *and* theories. In evaluating (positively) Festinger and Carlsmith's 1959 theory of 'cognitive dissonance' you might include a statement like:

> *Cognitive dissonance theory can help us understand aspects of consumer behaviour. If you buy a product you later come to dislike there may be a feeling of dissonance between your behaviour (buying) and your belief (dislike). A way of reducing this dissonance would be to convince yourself you like the product. This may explain why we're often so desperate to defend our purchases. We can take this a stage further. Festinger's theory would predict that the more we spend on a product we later dislike, the more likely we are to defend our purchase, since our feelings of dissonance will be greater than if we'd spent hardly anything. A greater understanding of consumer motivation is useful for shoppers and retailers.*

- **Androcentrism*** refers to gender issues in psychology. Like ethnocentrism, it's a form of prejudice. Research that doesn't recognise the viewpoint of women is seen as *androcentric*. Feminists have criticised psychology because of the high proportion of studies that use only male participants and whose findings are then generalised to *all* humans. Another manifestation of *androcentrism* is the tendency, amongst some psychologists, to regard issues that are especially relevant to men (for example, the relationship between television violence and aggression) as more mainstream to psychology, whilst issues that especially concern women (matters relating to pregnancy or breast self-examination) are seen as more peripheral and feature less often in the literature. Like *reductionism* and *ethnocentrism*, *androcentrism* is regarded as a negative feature of evidence.

In an essay, *androcentrism* can be used to evaluate studies *and* theories. In evaluating (negatively) Erikson's 1980 theory of lifecycle development, you might include a statement like:

> *Erikson's model is based solely on findings drawn from a male sample, yet he applies his theory of personality development to*

women as well as men. He even suggests that males and females approach the acquisition of 'ego identity' differently – females gaining identity via co-dependent sexual relationships, rather than in the more independent, masculine way (Gross, 1999). Applying a model researched only on men to all humans in this way is an example of androcentrism.

- **Method** refers to the way researchers carry out studies and collect data. There are a number of popular *methods* used by psychologists. Favourites include *controlled experiments, longitudinal studies, case studies, cross-cultural research, field experiments.* Some *methods* are closely associated with specific paradigms. Cognitive psychologists, for example, favour *controlled experiments.* Some *methods* are particularly suitable for ***measuring* aspects of participants' behaviour** and are referred to as **quantitative** methods (*controlled experiments* are an example). Others are better suited to ***describing* behaviour** and are referred to as **qualitative** methods (*case studies*). Still other methods can be *either* quantitative *or* qualitative, depending on how the researcher chooses to set up (or *design*) the study. When you're using this evaluation criterion bear in mind that *no method is better than another*. They all have their own strengths and weaknesses. This means that whatever study you're evaluating you should be critical *and* complimentary. See Chapter 3 for a more comprehensive review of *the methods in psychology.*

    In an essay, when evaluating (positively) the *method* of Freud's case of Little Hans you might include a statement like:

    > *The case study method provides a great deal of detail about a client. The researcher is able to develop a relationship with and an understanding of 'the whole person'. Studying the same person over a projected period also allows an understanding of developmental aspects of behaviour.*

- **Sample** refers to the participants used in psychological research. Ideally *samples* should be **representative**. This means they should **represent all the social groups that the results of the study are meant to apply to**. So if a study is about aggression in humans, yet it has an all-female sample, we can say it's *unrepresentative.* Representing *all* society's groups (twins, eccentrics, geniuses, etc.) in psychological research is an unrealistic aim, but researchers who cast their nets wide do produce more effective data. As well as representativeness, researchers should also go for *size*. A study that has a large sample will produce results that can be *generalised* to the rest of society with more confidence. Chapter 3 has more on *how to select a representative sample when carrying out research.*

In an essay, in evaluating (negatively) the *sample* Festinger and Carlsmith used in their 1959 study into 'cognitive dissonance' you might include a statement like:

> *Despite an elaborate, ingenious design this study is flawed because of its unrepresentative sample of 71 male psychology undergraduates from Stanford University. Where are the females? Where are the manual workers? Festinger and Carlsmith cannot confidently generalise their results to all groups in society after using such an unrepresentative sample.*

• **Socio-political impact*** refers to whether the research could be used to improve (or worsen) situations of inequality, exploitation or oppression. It may be that the results of a study could be taken up by a group in society who have experienced unfair treatment at the hands of those in power – oppressive regimes, tyrannical bosses. Alternatively, psychological evidence may be used by powerful groups to maintain unequal, exploitative states of affairs.

In an essay, when evaluating (negatively) the *socio-political impact* of Milgram's work on obedience, you might say:

> *Whilst this experiment tells us much about the human tendency towards 'doing as we're told', this is a worrying study in that its findings could be used by those who are in a position to elicit obedience in employees and prisoners. The socio-political impact of this could be to sustain oppressive regimes. More positively, the evidence could be used to help us understand how oppression arises, so that we might prevent it.*

Once you find your way around **the DRREEEEEAAAMSS system** you'll find some of the criteria to be *more relevant, more often* than others. *Extrapolation*, for example, is only really useful for studies using non-humans, whilst *Evidence* is handy in most evaluation situations. The key strength of **DRREEEEEAAAMSS** is that when you've used it a few times, when you've memorised and familiarised yourself with these 14 criteria, you can highlight the strengths and weaknesses of *any* study, *any* theory, in *any* psychology essay.

Evaluating studies and theories: the main points again

- It's almost unheard of to set essays that don't involve **evaluation**.
- Evaluation isn't just criticising. Be **complimentary** as well as critical.
- **DRREEEEEAAAMSS** gives you 14 criteria for evaluating psychological evidence.
- **DRREEEEEAAAMSS is a mnemonic** for helping you remember the 14 criteria.
- *Sometimes Adam And Eve Ran Absolutely Everywhere* helps you remember the 7 criteria for evaluating theories.

The last word

Your *knowledge* of psychology may have improved a little after reading this chapter. But what should really have improved are your *skills* for expressing your knowledge. The aim of Chapter 2 is to furnish you with some handy devices to help you learn the art of essay writing. If you use these devices regularly they should last you years. Here's a reminder of some of them:

- The *top ten* **instructions** used in psychology essay questions are *describe, evaluate, apply, discuss, define, explain, outline, compare, illustrate, analyse.*

- **Patterned essay planning** helps you plan your essays using networks of interrelated connections, rather than just lists.

- Wherever possible avoid using the words *prove, cause, right, believe, man, tribe, animals, subconscious, mental, subject.*

- **The DRREEEEEAAAMSS System** gives you 14 criteria for evaluating psychological evidence: *design, replicability, reductionism, ethics, ethnocentrism, ecological validity, extrapolation, evidence, approach, applicability, androcentrism, method, sample, socio-political impact.*

3 Skills for Doing Psychological Research

As well as introducing you to other people's research, sooner or later your psychology tutor will invite you to do a study of your own. There's nothing like doing research for helping you to appreciate how the studies you've read about turned out the way they did.

The decisions and compromises Milgram, Festinger, Freud and others made whilst doing their studies will make more sense to you after you've been through the research process yourself. On the other hand, some of their decisions might seem even more baffling.

Findings from famous psychology studies have a sort of cult status: the obedience level in Milgram's 1963 study: the conformity level in Solomon Asch's famous experiment in 1956: what Pavlov's dogs did in 1927. Anyone who's studied psychology – and some who haven't – can tell you something about the outcomes of these studies. Their *results* are famous and notorious, yet *how these results came about* is less well known.

As tutors and students we talk and write more about the results of studies than about the events that produced them. Milgram's experiment was a fascinating event in itself and it produced some fascinating findings. Events like these are planned and carried out on a day-to-day basis by researchers – sometimes painstakingly, sometimes ingeniously, sometimes with howling errors that nobody notices until months later.

Tough decisions and compromises have to be made about *what* to study, *who* to use as participants, *which* method to use, *how* to preserve the safety and dignity of everyone involved and *how* to encapsulate the study in the form of a **research report**. This chapter deals with each of these decisions and compromises. It's a practical guide to *doing* research. A user's manual to planning, carrying out and reporting research.

▶ Skill no. 1: Deciding what to study

Deciding what to study is about selecting a **research rationale**. A **research rationale** is a **statement of the aims of your research**. It points an inquiring finger at that 'gap in our understanding' of a topic (or aspect of a topic) that your research proposes to help us fill. Deciding on a workable research rationale can be a bit of a 'gazing blankly into space' experience. To keep this difficult gazing period to a minimum try taking your decision in little steps, rather than in one big leap.

Step 1   Choose a topic you're interested in
It's advisable to research into a topic you've studied on your course. Going 'away from home' is a gamble that can lead to quite a bit of extra work. So if you're fascinated by the psychology of serial killers or animal husbandry and neither of them appear on your syllabus, try to compromise. But within the limits of your course, *do choose something you're interested in*. Choose a topic (or aspect of a topic) that grabbed you when you did it in class. Or maybe go for something you've been reading about. Researching something you're indifferent to, or something you've been *told* to research because you haven't come up with an idea yourself, can be a real ball and chain. Especially when it comes to writing your **research report**.

I worked with a pair of students who nominated 'the formation of relationships' as their research topic. I'll use their example to illustrate how to put together a research rationale.

Step 2   Select a piece of evidence from your chosen topic
You've made your task more manageable by focusing on a single topic. Now it's time to get even more specific. From your topic, select a study or theory that you think is interesting *and* worthy of more investigation. When you have an idea in your sights, pause for a moment and ask yourself this question: *has anything already been written about this study or theory?*

If you can find some psychological evidence relating to the piece of research you've chosen, all well and good. You'll need to include relevant work from other authors when you write your research report. So check the course textbooks and make sure there's some material relating to the piece of evidence you've chosen *before you do your study*.

After reviewing work on 'the formation of relationships' our exemplar students, Sid and Nancy (names fictitious), chose Brown's Similarity Theory from 1986 as their area for research. This states that when we look for a partner or a friend, we're drawn to people who are of a similar level of attractiveness to ourselves. We tell ourselves 'All right, s/he might not be the most irresistible person I'll find, but s/he's the best I can realistically hope for.' We make a compromise, based on how attractive we think we are. A pretty interesting idea, reckoned Sid and Nancy, as well as being well documented in the course textbooks.

Step 3   Decide whether to replicate, modify or innovate
You've settled on an interesting (to you), fairly well-documented piece of evidence. This will be the launch-pad for your own study. Now you face three choices:

* *Choice 1* is to **do the study in the same way the original authors did it**. Or, in the case of a theory, to test it in the same way someone else has already tested it. This is called **replicating** research. And it's fine. It's a good way to verify the original findings and to see if they're *replicable* (see Chapter 2 for more on *replicability*).

* *Choice 2* is to **introduce a new element into the design of the original piece of research**. You do virtually the same study, with a new twist. You might, for instance, replace one variable with another. Let's say you find an original study about the influence of increased temperature levels on our ability to solve problems. Replace the word 'temperature' with 'noise' and you have a slightly different study. This is called **modifying** research. It's fine too. But there's a difference between *modifying* and *complicating*. By all means introduce a new element into the design of a study, but try not to make it any more complicated. Especially when you're just starting out in research.

* *Choice 3* brings with it rather surprising news. You may not realise it but many psychology courses don't reward originality in research design. If you come up with an original, groundbreaking idea for researching your topic you probably won't gain any more marks than you would if you'd done a replication. Yet whilst **innovation**

(**doing a study that isn't based on an original piece of research**) may not improve your grade, you shouldn't be put off from going ahead with it if there's an idea you really want to try, so long as it isn't a complicated idea. And so long as you can find evidence by other authors that relates to it.

Remember Sid and Nancy were using Brown's theory of relationship formation as the starting point for their research? Because they wanted to keep things simple they decided to replicate a fairly common method of testing the idea of similarity. They showed their participants a series of photographs of people they hadn't met, along with the instruction: 'Rate each one of these strangers on a 1–3 scale of how much you'd like to go on a date with them.' Then they showed the same participants the same photographs again and asked them to: 'Rate each of these strangers as more attractive, less attractive, or of a similar level of attractiveness as you are.' It's a common format for testing Brown's theory. The theory predicts that participants would rather go on a date with someone who they rate as 'roughly as attractive' as they themselves are.

Step 4   And finally, select your research rationale

So now you've really narrowed things down. You've selected a topic and a piece of research from your chosen topic. You've decided whether you're going to replicate or modify the research you've selected. You may even be intent on doing an original study. Now, finally, you're in a position to set out your research rationale.

Remember, your research rationale is your answer to the question: *'What's the aim of your study?'* It should be a clear, precise statement of the gap in our understanding that the results of your research will help us to fill. When you've decided how you're going to word it, pause for a moment and ask yourself a question: *'Is it really clear and precise?'* A good way to check this is to show it to someone and see how they react. If they read it, look at you and say: *'So what's the aim of your study then?'* you probably need to clarify things a little.

Sid and Nancy's research rationale looks like this: **A study to find out if we're more likely to ask for a date with someone we rate as 'about as attractive as we are' than we are to ask someone who we rate as 'more or less attractive' than we are.**

When you've settled on the wording for your *research rationale* you shouldn't find it too hard to convert it into a **testable prediction** about what you think the outcome of your study will be. This **testable**

prediction will be your **hypothesis** (see the opening section of Chapter 1 for a full discussion of hypotheses).

Sid and Nancy's rationale converts into a hypothesis that predicts: **Participants will be more likely to ask for a date with someone who they rate as 'about attractive as they are' than they are to ask someone who they rate as 'more or less attractive' than they are.**

Deciding what to study: the mains points again

- Select a topic to research that features on your syllabus.
- Select a research topic you're **interested** in.
- Find some established studies and theories relating to your research topic **before you do your study**.
- Many psychology courses **don't** award marks for originality in research design.
- Your research rationale should be a **clear**, **precise** statement of your aims.

Furnished with a clear **research rationale**, it's time now to settle on a **method**.

▶ Skill no. 2: Selecting your method

A **method** is a **way of carrying out research**. Once you've got your research rationale, your next job is to decide which method you're going to use. You'll be spoilt for choice, since there are plenty of alternatives. This section reviews the most popular and practical methods in psychology. The emphasis here is on those methods that lend themselves well to doing research for undergraduate psychology courses. It excludes several other methods that are either too expensive, too time-consuming or require too much training to be of very much use to anyone who's just starting out in research. You'll find a review of some of these other methods in Appendix 1 at the back of the book.

None of the popular, practical methods featured here is superior to any of the others. They all have advantages and disadvantages. Some, though, are more popular amongst psychology tutors and students than others. Also, some have more technical jargon attached to them than others do. In fact, **the controlled experiment** is the most popular method *and* it's the one that carries the most amount of jargon. Because of this you'll find more space devoted to it than to any of the other methods in the section that follows.

Method 1   Controlled experiments

Aren't they what chemists, physicists and biologists do?

Yes, and the ones they do have plenty in common with the ones psychologists do. For one thing, they do them in laboratories. So they're sometimes called **laboratory experiments**. For another thing, they follow '**The Rule of One Variable**', which states that:

> If two substances are treated in identical fashion in all respects except one, any difference in the outcome of those substances must be due to that one variable.

To illustrate this rule let's say you've prepared two samples of the same chemical in two separate test tubes, *A* and *B*. You apply a flame to each test tube. You get no reaction from either of them. Next, you add a measure of another chemical, *Z*, to test tube *B* and apply the flame to each test tube a second time. This time *B* bursts into flames. You'd probably conclude from this experiment that *B*'s bursting into flames was down to the introduction of *Z*. After all, *A* and *B* were treated in identical fashion *in all respects except this one*.

Controlled experiments in psychology work according to a similar principle. In a typical laboratory study you take two **groups** (or **conditions**, as psychologists call them) **of participants** and treat them identically *in all respects except one*. In other words, you try to ensure that your conditions are only treated differently according to *one variable*. This one variable is your **independent variable** (*IV*). It's **what separates *condition A* from *condition B***. It's sometimes called the **manipulated variable** because it's what you (the researcher) manipulate to ensure that it's *present* in one condition and *absent* in the other.

And the jargon doesn't end there.

We call the **condition where the *IV* is absent** the **control condition**, whilst the **condition where the *IV* is present** is called the **experimental condition**.

By the way, more adventurous researchers have three or four or more conditions in their experiments. Their *IV* would be absent in *condition A*, present in *B*, present to a greater degree in *C* and so on. But most undergraduate experiments stick to two conditions, so these are the ones I'm going to concentrate on in this discussion.

In 1968 Latane and Darley did a controlled experiment to investigate how people react in emergency situations. They created two conditions of participants, A and B. **One by one**, *participants in* condition A *were shown into a room and invited to sit down and fill in a questionnaire. Participants in* condition B *were shown into a similar room and invited to sit down and fill in a similar questionnaire* **as a group**. *In both conditions, after a few minutes, smoke billowed into the room through a grille in the wall. The researchers recorded participants' reaction time (how long it took them to raise the alarm).*

Have you spotted the *IV* in Latane and Darley's study? What's *present* in *condition B* (experimental condition), *absent* in *A* (control condition)? It's *other people*. They wanted to find out whether their participants would react to the emergency in a different way in a group setting, compared to when they were alone.

   Your independent variable (*IV*) is present in one condition, absent in the other. As an experimenter you're interested in the effect of the presence of your *IV* upon **some aspect of your participants' behaviour, which you'll observe and record during your experiment**. Latane and Darley were interested in the effect of their *IV* on their participants' *reaction time*. This aspect of behaviour – the one you observe and record in your experiment, the one that may be influenced by the presence or absence of the *IV* – is your **dependent variable** (*DV*). It's called this because its value may be *dependent* upon the presence or absence of your *independent variable*. To sum all this up, you could say that:

> Controlled experiments investigate the influence of an *IV* (the difference between two conditions) on a *DV* (some aspect of participants' behaviour).

What about those other types of variables, the ones that were featured in Chapter 1?

You mean **extraneous variables** (*EVs*). These *are* discussed in Chapter 1. There I said that a controlled experiment is a way of studying 'the effects of a change in one variable (*IV*) on the value of another (*DV*), whilst attempting to control all other extraneous variables'. You could say that **extraneous variables** are variables that break the *rule of one variable*. **Any variable that's present in one condition of an experiment and absent in the other** – *apart from the IV* – is regarded by experimenters as an *EV* that needs to be controlled, or, as we often put it, 'made constant' across the two conditions.

Latane and Darley were looking at the effect of other people (IV) on their participants' response time (DV). Condition A *were tested individually,* Condition B *were tested as a group. But what if* condition A *had consisted entirely of males and* B *had been all females? Here, gender would be an extraneous variable. The researchers would have to control it by making it constant across the conditions – by making sure they had equal numbers of males and females in* A *and* B*. Otherwise they would be unsure as to whether any differences in reaction time (between* A *and* B*) were due to gender or to the presence or absence of their* IV *(other people).*

As an experimenter you may feel as though you need eyes in the back of your head to keep a check on all the *EV*s that need to be controlled. But as Chapter 1 suggests, it's unrealistic to try to control *every conceivable extraneous variable* that might differ between the conditions of your experiment. Eye colour, intelligence, heart rate, fatigue . . . the list is endless. You can't control them all. But you *can* control the obvious ones. To help you decide which obvious ones to control, try dividing these *EV*s into two types: **extraneous *participant* variables** and **extraneous *situational* variables**.

> **Extraneous participant variables** (*EPV*s) are **characteristics of your *participants* that might vary between your conditions**. Gender and age are obvious examples. For example, the average age of your *condition A* might be ten years greater than in *condition B*.

> **Extraneous situational variables** (*ESV*s) are **aspects of the experimental setting that might vary between your conditions**. These include temperature, time of day, background noise and season. For example, you might test *condition A* in the morning and *B* in the afternoon.

As an experimenter your job is to control the effects of these *EV*s. As you design your experiment think about how you can make them constant between your conditions, so that your *rule of one variable* remains intact – so that your *IV* is the only thing that distinguishes *condition A* from *condition B*.

In an experiment like Latane and Darley's, time of day is an example of an ESV *that could be made constant across the conditions. A straightforward way of doing this would be to ensure that* conditions A *and* B *are both tested in the morning. This way you could be confident in linking any change in the* DV *to the* IV, *rather than to the fact that* condition B *was tested after a heavy lunch.*

Your most powerful tool for controlling troublesome *EVs* in your experiment is **how you divide participants into conditions**. There are three popular methods for doing this, or **experimental designs**, as proper psychologists call them.

> **The Independent Design** has **no participant appearing in more than one condition** of the experiment. *Conditions A and B* have entirely different *personnel*, though they usually have equal *numbers* of participants.

> **The Repeated Measures Design** has **all participants appearing in both conditions**. So if you're a participant in an experiment with this kind of design you'll be observed twice, in *condition A and* in *B*.

> In **the Matched Pairs Design** the experimenter pre-tests participants *in relation to the extraneous variable she's aiming to control*. If she's trying to control the *EV* of *age*, she'll find out how old each participant is before dividing everyone up. If she's trying to control *intelligence* she'll give all the participants an IQ test before dividing them up. Armed with this data she'll then make sure that an equal number of old and young (or *high* and *low IQ achievers*) appear in each condition. A good way of doing this is by ranking the participants from *eldest* to *youngest* (or *highest to lowest IQ*), then putting the eldest in *condition A*, the second eldest in *condition B*, the third eldest in *A* and so on. Matched pairs designs are like *Independent Designs* in that no one appears in more than one condition of the experiment.

Latane and Darley could have used any of these designs for their experiment. An Independent Design would have had condition A *filling in their questionnaires individually and* condition B *filling theirs in as a* group. In a Repeated Measures Design, the same participants would have filled in the questionnaire twice: once alone, once as a group. A Matched Pairs Design would have had all the participants being pre-tested on (for example) intelligence. Equal numbers of high and low achievers would then be put in two groups, A and B, in an effort to make the EPV of intelligence constant across the two conditions. However, as **Box 3A** suggests, matching participants in this way doesn't eliminate EPVs, though it does help to reduce their effect.

As **Box 3A** shows, none of these three designs is better than another. They all have advantages and problems.

What's **counterbalancing**?

Counterbalancing is **a way of dealing with 'the order effect' in experiments that have a Repeated Measures Design**. Let's say you've set up an experiment in which all participants appear in conditions A and B. And let's say they all appear in A first, then B. Chances are they'll either become fatigued or practised as the experiment wears on. This means they'll either do worse in B (fatigue) or better in B (practice) partly for reasons that have nothing to do with the absence or presence of the IV. Rather, because of the order in which they appeared in the two conditions.

If everyone in Latane and Darley's experiment appeared in condition A (alone) first, then condition B (group), they may have reacted faster in B because it was their second emergency of the day. They'd had practice. Their reaction time (DV) was dependent not only on the presence or absence of other people (IV), but also on the order in which they appeared in the two conditions (ESV).

In situations like this order is an extraneous situational variable. It's your job as the experimenter to try and make ESVs like this constant between your two conditions. This is where counterbalancing comes in.

If your Repeated Measures experiment is susceptible to the order effect, divide your participants into two equal groups. Let the first group appear in condition A first, then B. Let the second group appear in B first, then A. This will neutralise the fatigue and practice effects. They'll still be present, but now they'll move in two directions, rather than just one. To put this another way – half your participants will be fatigued in A, half in B; half will be practised in A, half in B.

Box 3A All three experimental designs have advantages and problems

	An advantage of this design is . . .	A problem with this design is . . .
The Independent Design	. . . that because your participants only appear in one condition there are no **order effects**. . . . that participants are less likely to display **demand characteristics**. As they're only tested once, they have less opportunity to 'work out' the aims of the experiment.	. . . **participant variables** (*PVs*). All participants have different characteristics and abilities. In Independent Designs some *PVs* will vary across conditions. Variables like intelligence, self-esteem (and many others) will be more in evidence in one condition than in the other. The unequal distribution of these *PVs* between the conditions will ensure that the rule of one variable will always be bent a little. . . . that you **need more participants** than you do in Repeated Measures designs, since each participant only produces one set of data.
The Repeated Measures Design	. . . that you **need fewer participants** than you do in the other designs, since everyone is observed and tested twice. Effectively, you get two sets of data for the price of one participant. . . . that you don't have the problem of **participant variables** (*PVs*).	. . . the **order effect**. This is a consequence of having participants that appear in both conditions. The order effect comes in two varieties. **First**, the **fatigue effect**. This is when your participants grow tired or bored. Their performance deteriorates the longer your study goes on. **Second**, the **practice effect**. Here, participants grow more comfortable with their setting (or more competent at the tasks they're given). Their performance improves as the experiment goes on. Both these effects produce

	Participants are effectively being compared with themselves, so there are no characteristics or abilities that vary across the conditions.	performances that vary between conditions for reasons other than the presence or absence of the *IV*. So the rule of one variable is broken. You can deal with the **order effect** by **counterbalancing** (there's an explanation of this coming up). ... **demand characteristics** (*DCs*). This is when participants guess what the experimenter expects from the outcome of the study. They react in one of two ways. **Either** they try to make the study work out' the way the experimenter expects it to. **Or** they try to prevent the experimenter's expectations being fulfilled. As with the order effects, *DCs* produce behaviours that vary between your two conditions.
The Matched Pairs Design	... the reduced effects of participant variables. Pre-testing participants on one or more *PV* reduces the degree to which they vary between conditions. ... as with the Independent Design, order effects don't present a problem because your participants only appear in one condition.	... even though you've pre-tested your participants (on one or more *PV*) and divided them into conditions accordingly, the *PV* will still be a thorn in your side, for two reasons. **First** there will still be some variation between the two groups, even on the variables you've pre-tested. **Second**, there will still be a number of variables you haven't pre-tested for and these will vary between conditions. ... that compared to the other two designs, the pre-testing procedure makes this is a fairly time-consuming business.

Now you can be more confident in claiming that any differences in the behaviour of your two conditions, *A* and *B*, are due to the presence or absence or your *IV*, rather than to the *order* in which they appeared in the two conditions. The precise name for this method of controlling *the order effect* is **ABBA counterbalancing** (since half your participants appear in *A then B* and half in *B then A*). It's a handy device but it isn't perfect. It won't eliminate fatigue or practice from your experiment, though it will help you to control their effects.

If Latane and Darley's study were done as a Repeated Measures Experiment, ABBA counterbalancing would be a handy device for controlling the order effect. If half the participants appeared in A *then* B *and half in* B *then* A *the effect of 'practice' would be neutralised. It would affect performances in both conditions equally.*

You have to make compromises when you do controlled experiments in psychology. You're investigating the influence of one kind of variable (*IV*) on another kind of variable (*DV*), whilst trying to make a third class of variables (*EV*) constant across your conditions. Realistically you can't control every extraneous variable that threatens to bend or break the *rule of one variable* in your experiment. But don't lose hope. You're not entirely powerless. Controlled experiments got their name because they incorporate a number of handy tools to help you stay in charge of your research. *Independent, Repeated Measures* and *Matched Pairs Designs*, as well as *ABBA counterbalancing*, can all help you deal with troublesome *EVs*, so that when you record a difference in the behaviour of your two conditions you can confidently trace it back to your *IV*, rather than to some other, extraneous feature of your experiment.

Your job as experimenter is to select the most appropriate tools for your research project. The ones I've featured in this section are all pretty handy, though they're not *power*-tools. They won't *eliminate* extraneous variables from your experiment, though they will help you to control their effects.

Controlled experiments are part of an overall approach to doing psychological research, called the **quantitative** approach. Psychologists who adopt this approach **observe behaviour**, then they tend to **express their observations in a *numerical* form**. In other words, they produce *measurements* of behaviour, using graphs, tables, percentages. Doing research like this enables you to make comparisons between your participants' behaviour. Take Latane and Darley, for instance. Their results were expressed in seconds and minutes. They were *measuring* their participants' reaction time. The alternative to the quantitative approach in psychology is called the **qualitative**. The next section, on **case studies**, has more on this.

Advantages of controlled experiments

Doing research in laboratories gives you **control** over a lot of the variables that influence what happens in your study. In your laboratory (or in the classroom you're using as your laboratory) you can vary and manipulate lots of variables you'd have no control over if you were working in a naturalistic setting. *You* select the lighting, the noise level, how many people there are in the room. It's up to you if you want to make any of these variables constant across your conditions. Being in **control** is what draws people to this method.

Because of the amount of control they offer, laboratory experiments are highly **replicable** (see Chapter 2 for a discussion of **replicability**). It's an asset if your study can be repeated (*replicated*) by another researcher (or by you yourself) at a later date, as it means that your original findings can be checked or verified. Because laboratory experimenters manipulate so many of their variables themselves, their studies are relatively easy to replicate – more so than studies that take place in naturalistic settings, where you'd have a difficult job reproducing the exact temperature, noise or crowding levels of the original research.

Controlling your experimental variables means you can use a **standardised** procedure in your experiment. As far as you can, you need to make sure that all your participants are treated in the same way. This means giving the same instructions, with the same wording, the same amount of guidance, to everyone. Variations in how participants are treated will act as an **extraneous variable**, so it should be avoided. In a laboratory, where you can rehearse your procedure down to the last detail, you're less likely to fall into the trap of *treating some people more equally than others*.

Disadvantages of controlled experiments

One disadvantage is **ecological validity**. You should be getting used to this term now. It features in Chapters 1 and 2, so I won't labour the point again. In short, the argument goes like this. Findings from laboratory experiments can't help us to understand how we behave in everyday settings because they're too artificial. They *lack ecological validity*. The laboratory *setting* is artificial, which leads participants to behave unnaturally. The *tasks* researchers ask participants to do in laboratory studies are also artificial, again leading to unnatural reactions.

Watch out too for **demand characteristics**. These are particular problems in *Repeated Measures* experiments, where participants are being observed for a longer period of time, but they can crop up in all experiments. When participants know what the aim of your study is they may influence its outcome, consciously or otherwise. They may try to make the experiment 'work out' like (they think) the experimenter wants it to. Or else they'll try to sabotage its outcome to upset the experimenter's expectations. Influences like these will act as *extraneous variables*, so prevent them where you can. A good way of outlawing demand characteristics is to ensure your participants don't find out what the aim of your study is. Mind you, deceiving your participants like this could leave you open to cries of 'unethical'. (There will be more on these ethical dilemmas later in this chapter.)

A related problem is **experimenter bias**. This can happen when *the researcher* knows the experiment's aims. Knowing what's expected to happen s/he might – consciously or otherwise – influence its outcome to conform with these expectations. S/he may even communicate these expectations to the participants (consciously or otherwise), which would lead to *demand characteristics*. A good way of combating *experimenter bias* is to use competent researchers to carry out the study who are ignorant of its aims and of what its outcome is expected to be. Experimenters who are kept naive in this way are usually referred to as **blind researchers**.

Controlled experiments are the most complicated of the methods included in this chapter, so if you've understood this part of the chapter you should be all right with the rest of it. Before you move on, pause for a moment and make sure you know what these terms mean:

- **the rule of one variable**
- **control** and **experimental conditions**
- **independent, dependent** and **extraneous variables**
- **independent, repeated measures** and **matched pairs designs**
- **the order effect**
- **demand characteristics**
- **ABBA counterbalancing**
- **standardised procedures**
- **experimenter bias**
- **blind researchers**

Method 2   Case studies

After studying the behaviour of Trobriand Islanders – to the east of New Guinea – in the 1920s, Bronislaw Malinowski came to the conclusion that 'although people feel or think or experience certain psychological states in association with the performance of customary acts, the majority of them surely are not able to put them into words' (1922). In another words, people aren't very good at 'speaking their minds'. This is rotten news for psychologists. How are we supposed to study what people think, feel and experience if we can't rely on what they tell us about their thoughts, feelings, experiences? Malinowski called this question 'the real Gordian knot of social psychology' (a Gordian knot is a type of knot that's hard to untie).

Case studies are deeply entangled in Malinowski's knot because they involve psychologists asking people to talk about their feelings, thoughts, experiences. They also involve observing and recording people's *behaviour*. Doing case studies means making a combined record of what people say *and* do.

So how would you define a case study?

It's **a detailed study of an individual or group**. Usually you're looking in detail at *one* person's life, past and present. Detail – the idea of looking at the small print of someone's thoughts, feelings, experiences – is the essence of the case study. More so than with any other method, case studies allow you to get 'close up' to the person you're studying, so that you can arrive at an intimate portrait of them, their relationships, desires, weaknesses, strengths etc.

Case studies are part of an overall approach to doing psychological research called the **qualitative** approach. Psychologists who do qualitative research aren't satisfied with observing and recording people's *behaviour*, they want to know how people *feel* about their behaviour, too. They want to know about the meanings people attach to what they do.

Let's say, for example, you notice that your next-door neighbour has a habit of talking to himself. If you were taking a qualitative approach to researching this problem, you wouldn't just record his behaviour, you'd go next door and ask him to tell you about what he was doing. As Malinowski put it, you'd try to grasp 'his vision of his world' (1922). In effect, you'd do a case study.

In The Man Who Mistook His Wife for a Hat *(1985) Oliver Sacks reports on his case study of Ray. From his conversations and observations Sacks tells the story of Ray's experience of Tourette's Syndrome – a neurologi-cal condition that leaves the individual with a number of uncontrollable tics, jerks and twitches. Sacks argues that in some ways Tourette's is the flipside of Parkinson's disease, since 'Touretters' have an excess of the same excitor transmitter in the brain that 'Parkinsonians' lack. Where the Parkinsonian is lethargic, the Touretter is frenetic. The case study of 'Witty Ticcy Ray' is an intimate record of Ray's behaviour and of how he feels about his Tourettism.*

Different researchers do case studies for different reasons. Bilton (1996) makes a distinction between **idiographic** and **indicative** case studies.

Researchers who do **idiographic** studies are interested in a parti-cular case because of its outstanding, unique qualities. **Idiographic** is a handy term to learn because it figures fairly often elsewhere in psychology. It means **referring to the unique qualities of an indi-vidual**. Authors of studies like these aren't so interested in shedding light on *people's behaviour in general* from what they've found out about their particular case. They're simply saying 'Look, this case is unique and interesting'.

The aim of doing **indicative** case studies is to enlighten us about people *generally*. Here, the author feels that knowing more about their case – or an aspect of their case's life – will help us understand more about human behaviour in general. Another way of putting this is that the insights gained from **indicative** case studies are **generalisable to other cases and situations**.

Sacks's case of Ray tells us more about the inner world of the Touret-ter. A quote from Ray himself illustrates this: 'You "normals", who have the right transmitters in the right places at the right times in your brains, have all feelings, all styles, available all the time – gravity, levity, what-ever is appropriate. We Touretters don't . . .' Listening to Ray talk about his condition helps Sacks to understand how unpredictable the experi-ence of Tourette's syndrome is. The case of Ray 'in particular' helps us to unravel Tourettes 'in general'. In this sense, Sacks takes an indicative approach.

Doing case studies effectively

This involves negotiating a number of carefully laid traps. All methods have their own particular pitfalls. The trap you're most likely to stumble into when you do a case study is **the partiality trap**. This relates to the *subjective* viewpoint of you, the researcher. Here are some pointers on how to recognise it and then step over it.

When you're studying a participant 'close up' there's a danger that instead of reporting what s/he *actually* says and does, you'll report *your interpretation* of what s/he says and does. This can happen consciously or unconsciously. There's a greater danger of this when you have certain *expectations* about what s/he's doing or why s/he's doing it. It's all too easy to find yourself reporting behaviour *the way you see it*, rather than *the way your participant intends it to be seen*. You might, for instance, report a throwaway comment as a 'scathing aside'.

This kind of *partiality* is especially characteristic of the case study method. You could say it's the case study equivalent of 'experimenter bias'. Earlier in this chapter (in the section on controlled experiments) I suggested using 'blind' (uninformed) researchers as a technique for reducing the effects of experimenter bias. This isn't really appropriate in a case study setting. If you're making a detailed portrait of your participant's thoughts, feelings and experiences, it's a good thing if you *and* your participant are familiar with the aims of the research. But don't despair. There are ways of avoiding **the partiality trap** when you're doing a case study. Here are three of them:

1 *Be honest* about when you're being impartial and when you're not (Coolican, 1996). In your report, make it clear when you're offering your interpretation of what your participant said and did and when you're simply describing events *as they happened*. You might use phrases like 'it seemed to me that . . .' or 'you could say that . . .' where you're giving your own views.

2 *Quote your participant* (Coolican, 1996). Including, as Sacks did in the case of Ray, some direct statements from the person you're studying, adds credibility to your report. A direct, unadulterated transcription of something your participant actually said is less partial than your version of what they said.

3 *'Touch base'* (Bilton et al., 1996). Good practice in qualitative research means involving your participant in the reporting process. There's no one better to check the accuracy of what you're reporting than your participant. As you gather your notes, show them to your participants and ask them if you're giving a fair representation of what they've been saying and doing.

When you're doing qualitative research it's impossible to banish your own interpretations from your report altogether – they're bound to creep in. *Being honest, quoting your participant* and *touching base* won't *eliminate* partiality from your case study, though they will help you to reduce its effects.

Advantages of case studies

Researchers are drawn to the case study method because of the level of **detail** it yields about a participant. You'll gather more data about a single participant by doing a case study than you would using any other method. You'll be able to spend a good deal of time with your participant, so you'll be able to observe them in a variety of situations and speak to them about a variety of their thoughts, feelings and experiences.

Case studies allow you a good deal of **flexibility**. It may be that during your discussions with your participant you stumble upon something about them that you want to follow up. S/he may turn out to be a twin, or a war veteran, or an arachnaphobic. When you're doing a case study you're free to follow up these new lines of inquiry because you don't set out with a rigid, clearly stated research rationale. The aims of case studies tend to be more 'open-ended'.

Disadvantages of case studies

Unlike controlled experiments, case studies are **not replicable**. Once you've done a case study you can't do the same study again, either with the same participant or with a different one. As a researcher doing a case study you have a lot of contact with your participant. You ask numerous questions, you make numerous observations. You enter into numerous complex interactions that can never be repeated.

Because they are unique, the findings from case studies are **hard to generalise**. Although you might find out a lot about a particular participant, you'd be hard pressed to say with any confidence that your findings tell us much about the rest of the population. This is the disadvantage of doing a study that only has one participant. S/he might, after all, be pretty unusual. No matter what you discover about him/her, it may tell us nothing about the rest of us. This is a real drawback if you're attempting to do an 'indicative' case study.

Method 3   Questionnaires

GQ, *Country Life*, *Jinty*, they're all at it. Your average weekly magazine would seem incomplete without a questionnaire for its readers to complete. They're good news for people with long train journeys ahead of them and they're good news for psychologists, who want to collect lots of data about a large sample of participants without spending very much time, effort or money. Whatever magazine takes your fancy, you'll know that filling in questionnaires is straightforward enough. What you might not realise is that making them up is a bit of a puzzle. This section suggests some solutions.

How would you define a questionnaire?

It is defined as **a set of written questions to be answered by respondents**. In some studies the researchers are around whilst respondents fill in their answers – these are called *face-to-face* questionnaires. In others the researchers hand over the questionnaires, then leave the respondents to get on with it – these are called *self-completion* questionnaires. In a third category – *postal* questionnaires – respondents never even meet the researchers. They receive them, fill them in and send them back by post or e-mail.

Lapiere did a study in 1934 using a postal questionnaire. He drove 10,000 miles across the USA with a young Chinese couple, calling at hotels to ask for rooms. Out of 67 hotels, 66 gave them a warm welcome, leaving Lapiere with the view that racist attitudes towards Chinese minorities were a rarity in the USA. Six months later Lapiere sent the same hotels a questionnaire asking – amongst other things – if they'd let rooms to Chinese people. Guess what: 92 per cent said 'no'. Lapiere had to rethink his optimistic view about racist attitudes. It's also worth noting that only 51 per cent of hoteliers bothered to send back their questionnaires.

The questions on questionnaires are often called *items*. They come in two varieties – **closed** and **open-ended** items.

Closed items are child's play for respondents. They come complete with *suggested responses*. All they have to do is pick one. Typical *suggested responses* are 'yes', 'no' and 'don't know'. A variation on this theme involves providing a scale of 1–7 and asking respondents to say how much they agree with a statement, like, for example, 'the earth is flat'. A response of 1 usually means 'I don't agree at all', whereas 7 means 'I totally agree'. This kind of 1–7 method is called a Likert scale, after its inventor.

*Are questionnaires **quantitative** or **qualitative**?*

They can be either. **Open-ended** items are an example of *qualitative* research. Here, items come *minus* suggested responses. Respondents have to make up their own, which means they have more work to do. On the plus side, it also means you get more detailed information about your respondents. Open-ended items are useful if you're interested in your respondents' views and opinions about a certain issue.

Closed items allow you to gather your data in *numerical* form. You can work out *how many* people said 'yes', 'no' and 'don't know' to each item. If you're using a Likert scale you can work out – numerically – how strongly your participants agree with the statement that 'the earth is flat'. Collecting data numerically like this is an example of the *quantitative* approach.

Lapiere was assessing racism quantitatively. He was representing racist attitudes amongst his respondents numerically, using percentages. A more qualitative approach would have involved using a questionnaire item asking respondents to describe their attitudes towards Chinese tourists. This would have yielded a more detailed representation of their attitudes.

Writing questionnaires effectively

This is a fine art. A well-written questionnaire with carefully crafted items can make the difference between doing effective and ineffective research. As you sit down to write your questionnaire, be on the look-out for some cunningly placed traps. Here are five of them, along with some strategies for side-stepping them.

The 'throwing them in at the deep end' trap Anyone who's filled in a questionnaire knows that motivation amongst respondents is generally pretty low. As a rule, respondents are a lethargic bunch who are easily distracted from their task. Consequently they need to be wined and dined a little. With this in mind the first item on your questionnaire is critical. Don't throw your respondents in at the deep end. Make *item 1* nice and easy. *Item 1* isn't there to yield data, it's there to welcome your respondents to your questionnaire and coax them towards *item 2*.

The 'irrelevance trap' In the world of the questionnaire less is most definitely more. Effective questionnaires are short and sweet. Remember that respondents lack stamina. Including items that don't relate to your *research rationale* is seriously frowned upon.

The 'terminology' trap Think back to Chapter 2. Do you remember what *'psychology words'* are? They're words that only make sense to people who've studied psychology. They're jargon or technical terms that need explaining to non-psychologists. Including 'psychology words' in questionnaire items is like shooting yourself in the foot. Your respondents – who, remember, are in a state of low motivation in any case – will wander off and do something else as soon as they stumble across an item they don't understand. This problem is magnified if you're using *self-completion* questionnaires, where there's no one around to help with any difficulties. Avoid the trap: write plainly.

The 'leading questions' trap Questionnaire respondents, like many of us, are easily led. Consequently you need to make sure you don't lead them towards making unnatural responses because of the way you phrase your items. Use *neutral* phrases like *Is the earth flat or spherical?* rather than leading phrases like *Do you agree that the earth is flat?* Also, if you're using *closed* items be sure to provide a healthy variety of *possible responses*. A choice of 'yes' or 'no' is often not enough. 'Don't know' is a popular answer to many questions. How many times have you used it today?

The 'lies, fraud and mischief' trap I'm not saying people who fill in questionnaires are liars. However, they don't always give entirely honest responses. As a researcher there isn't a lot you can do about this, though including a *lie detector* in your questionnaire might help. Put in two items that ask the same question using different wording. For example, *item 3* could say *Is the earth flat or spherical?* and *item 5* could say *Is the earth shaped more like a pancake or a beach ball?* It's a fair bet that anyone who gives conflicting responses to these items is either lying, fraudulent or mischievous (not taking your questionnaire seriously). So you can discard their responses.

Advantages of questionnaires

Questionnaires are excellent for **reaching inaccessible respondents**. When you're doing research it's sometimes hard to find a time and a place to meet your participants to carry out your study. Questionnaires offer you a solution to this problem. You can distribute them in one meeting (or with no meetings at all, if you post or e-mail them) and whilst you're at it you can agree on a deadline for their return. When you're dealing with respondents who are either busy or a long way away this is a real advantage for your research project.

When you do a questionnaire study you're more or less guaranteed of having a **standardised procedure**. In other words, it's easy for you to ensure that all your respondents are treated equally because your instructions and your items are incorporated onto the questionnaire itself. So there's little danger of some respondents being treated 'more equally than others'.

Disadvantages of questionnaires

Asking someone to write down what they'd do in a certain situation is no substitute for *observing* what they do when they're actually out there, in that situation. Do you always do what you say you'll do? No, neither do I. The problem with questionnaires is that you're asking people to respond to **hypothetical items**. And even the most honest, diligent respondent is likely to say one thing and do another.

As Lapiere discovered in his study, the **response rate** to questionnaires can be pretty low. And of the ones you do get back, some will be only half filled-in or may have to be discarded because of the *lie detector*. This is a particular problem with postal, e-mail and self-completion questionnaires.

Method 4   Field studies

Asking someone to write down what they'd do in a certain situation is no substitute for observing what they do when they're actually out there, in the situation (or *in the field*, as most researchers would put it). You yourself may be one of those researchers who feels that so many people 'speak with forked tongues' about their thoughts, feelings and experiences that doing a questionnaire study isn't worth the bother. You'd rather observe what people *actually* do than read about what they *intend* to do. You may also be one of those researchers who sees little point in observing and recording behaviour in laboratories, since all you get are *artificial* responses to *artificial* requests.

If some of these views sound like yours, don't lose heart. There is a method that may suit you down to the ground: **field studies**.

How do you define a field study?

It is defined as **a piece of research that takes place in a natural setting**. Its aim is to take your research to your participants, rather than bringing them into your laboratory to be studied. This means you can observe and record *everyday behaviour in everyday settings*. After all, psychology should help us to understand the *ordinary* things we do, not just the things we do in unusual, highly controlled situations. Another way of putting this is to say that doing field studies helps you improve the *ecological validity* of your research (see Chapter 2 for more on this). Field studies come in two varieties.

1   Field experiments

These are controlled experiments, with one difference. As in laboratory experiments you study **the effects of a change in one variable (*IV*) on the value of another (*DV*), whilst attempting to control all other extraneous variables**, but here you do it *in a natural setting*. You give up the warmth and predictability of your laboratory for the cold, wet unpredictability of the outside world – *the field*. Popular venues for doing field experiments are restaurants, schools and public conveniences. You can do them wherever there are participants to be studied.

Most of what appears in the section earlier in this chapter on controlled experiments also applies to field experiments, so I won't dwell on them. But they do have a couple of distinguishing features that ought to make you pause for thought before using this method.

Firstly, because you're aiming to study *everyday behaviour in everyday settings* you can't really tell your participants they're being studied. Would *you* act naturally if someone told you you were in a psychology experiment? No. So field experiments tend to be done **covertly – without the participants knowing they're being studied**. Other methods use covert methods too, but field experiments use them more often than most.

Secondly, because you've sacrificed the warm predictability of your laboratory for the cold, erratic, outside world, you'll find **extraneous variables** harder to control. When you do a field experiment you're at the mercy of the elements far more than you are in your laboratory, where temperature, lighting and who's around are in your control. The upshot of this is that some of these extraneous variables will vary between your conditions, thus bending your *rule of one variable* (see the section on controlled experiments for a full explanation of this rule).

Middlemist et al. *did their research in a public toilet (research cited in Bell* et al., *1996). Their field experiment – done in a Gents in 1976 – investigated the effect of having someone standing next to you on physiological arousal, which was measured by timing how long participants took to start urinating.* Condition A *had a confederate standing at the next urinal to the unsuspecting participant.* Condition B *had the confederate standing three urinals away. Another researcher hid in a cubicle with a home-made periscope and a stopwatch to record how long it took each participant to begin. The researchers found that having someone close by increased arousal, thus delaying urination. In this experiment the IV was the distance between the participant and the confederate, the DV was how long it took the participant to urinate.*

*Are field experiments **quantitative** or **qualitative**?*

Like laboratory experiments, they tend to err on the *quantitative* side, though researchers who use this method often design their studies so they collect a mixture of the two types of data.

2 Field observations

These involve **making a record of events and behaviour that take place in a natural setting**. Sometimes they're called 'non-experimental observations' to distinguish them from field experiments. There are no *IV*s, *DV*s, *EV*s or conditions in field observations. You could say that they're a more straightforward way of recording *everyday behaviour in everyday settings*. You don't have to worry about controlling or manipulating variables when you're using this method, though there are still a few preliminaries you should observe before you start your field observations.

There are two types of field observations. The first – **participant observation** – isn't especially popular with students who've recently begun doing research in psychology as it requires a little more time and training than you may have access to at this early stage in your research career. Nontheless, it's well worth knowing about.

Participant observation involves **gaining entry into and sharing the experiences of the group of participants you're studying, whilst at the same time gathering *qualitative* data**. The participant observer lives a kind of double life, participating in the life of the group as well as making descriptive observations, gathering field notes. Participant observation studies have famously been carried out in hospitals, on kibbutzim and even amongst street gangs. This method – often called **ethnography** – is much used by social anthropologists and can be carried out either overtly or covertly.

In 1973 a team of researchers led by Rosenhan bluffed their way into a number of psychiatric wards by inventing minor schizophrenic symptoms (see Rosenhan, 1973). Once inside, they carried out covert participant observations into the daily interactions between patients and medical staff. The resulting paper, 'On being sane in insane places', startled the psychiatric profession on two counts. First, it highlighted how easy it was to be committed to a psychiatric ward: all you had to do was say you were 'hearing voices'. Second, it highlighted how difficult it was to persuade medical staff that you were sane enough to get out. In some cases it took weeks for the researchers to extricate themselves.

A more popular choice for psychology undergraduates is the second type of field observation – **non-participant observation**. Whilst *participant observation* involves studying a group from the inside, **non-participant observation** is about being on the outside looking in. It involves **making a record of events and behaviour that take place in a natural setting, *without becoming part of the group you're studying***.

Non-participant observation can be done *overtly* (where participants know they're being studied) or *covertly* (where they don't). There are positive and negative sides to each of these. Studying participants overtly can produce *demand characteristics* (the section on controlled experiments earlier in this chapter has an explanation of these), whilst covert research raises *ethical* issues (see the section on ethics later in this chapter for more on these).

*Are field observations **qualitative** or **quantitative**?*

They can be either. Doing them *quantitatively* involves observing participants' behaviour and recording it in a *numerical* form. Researchers who do *quantitative* observations use a technique called *systematic observation*, which is explained below. Doing *qualitative* observation involves recording behaviour in a descriptive way. This method is favoured by researchers who prefer to use a *participant observation* method.

In 1958 Bales did a non-participant observation of the communication styles of groups who make decisions (see Bales, 1958). Concealed behind a one-way mirror, researchers looked out for and recorded a selection of behaviours such as 'showing solidarity', 'giving opinions', 'showing tension'. Results were presented in a numerical form, showing how important each type of behaviour was as a percentage of overall communication. For example, they found that 56 per cent of all communicative acts fell into the category of 'attempting to solve a problem'. Clearly, Bales was collecting data quantitatively. Participants in this study knew they were being observed, making it an overt observation.

Wait! Aren't there a lot of different types of field studies?

It may seem so, though actually, no. But if it's bothering you, pause for a moment and take a look at **Box 3B**, which should clear things up a little.

As I have already said, *field experiments* are really a version of *controlled experiments*, so for tips on how to do them go back to the section that deals with that method earlier in this chapter. As I also mentioned, doing *participant observations* tends to be beyond the scope of undergraduate psychology students, but here are some tips on how to deal with *non-participant observations*.

Doing non-participant observations effectively
This involves treading carefully to avoid a number of smartly positioned traps. Here are some especially notorious ones, along with some tips for bypassing them.

The 'no system' trap You can't record everything about your

Box 3B Field studies come in a variety of types

Variety 1 Field experiments	Variety 2 Field observations
You study the effects of a change in one variable (*IV*) on the value of another (*DV*), whilst attempting to control all other extraneous variables, in a natural setting.	You make a record of events and behaviour in a natural setting. They can be done *covertly* or *overtly*.
Field experiments are like controlled experiments, except they take place in 'the real world'. They tend to be done *covertly*.	**Type 1 Participant observation**, where you join the group you're studying. **Type 2 Non-participant observation**, where you collect your data without becoming part of the group you're studying.

participants' behaviour; some things will escape your notice. Nor is it a good idea to determine to record *as much you can* of what your participants do. Doing this will leave too much open to your own subjectivity – the way *you* see things. An alternative approach is to devise a *system for observation* – decide on certain *prescribed behaviour/s* to focus on and record *these and these only*. Be sure that the prescribed behaviours you focus on are *easy to recognise* and *easy to define*. This will make them easier to record. For example, recording 'finger pointing' is easier to spot than, say, 'flirting', which is famously hard to define. Suppose you do decide to record 'finger pointing' outside the window of your local toyshop. There are a number of ways you could do this. You could count the number of 'finger-points' in an hour. You could compare males with females on 'finger pointing'. You could measure the average duration of a 'finger-point'. Any of these would be fine, since you'd be observing a prescribed behaviour that's *easy to recognise, easy to define* and therefore easy to record. This strategy of **focusing on a prescribed behaviour, then recording it numerically** is called **systematic observation**.

The 'no tapes' trap Having a tape of what happened during your observation session is a useful back-up when you're analysing your data. During your study you're likely to miss or misunderstand some of the things your participants say and do. If you record what happened onto video or audio tape you can go back and clarify ambiguities. A word of warning, though. Recording participants' behaviour should only be done with their consent, so this is a luxury that's restricted to *overt* research.

The 'lone-observer' trap Doing an observation on your own means trusting yourself to be competent enough to make an accurate record of what your participants say and do. This is a big responsibility. You can relieve some of it by having two or more observers working independently (so as not to influence each other during the observation session). You'll probably find that even though they'll be dealing with *prescribed behaviours* – so they'll know what they're looking out for – your observers will still produce slightly differing accounts of what went on. This is inevitable – everyone has their own interpretation of events. But if your observers produce *extravagantly* differing records it might be worth checking a few aspects of the design of your study. Are your observers *really* clear about their roles? Are they *really* focusing on prescribed behaviours that are easy to define? Did they *really* attend the same observation session?

The 'blowing cover' trap If you're doing *covert* research try not to *look and behave like people who are doing psychological* *research*. Avoid appearing shifty, standing around with notepads, discussing the ins and outs of your study within earshot of your participants – that kind of thing. If you draw attention to yourself your participant may not realise you're doing psychological research, but they may well think something's not quite right. This may lead them to behave unnaturally, which is precisely what you don't want. So keep a low profile.

If you're doing *overt* research it's still worth keeping a low profile. Although your participants know they're being studied, this won't be uppermost in their minds throughout the entire session. After a few minutes of uncertainty they'll probably forget about you and get on with whatever they're doing. So once the observation is underway try to blend into the background. Keep quiet, avoid rustling, scribbling and fiddling with tapes, stopwatches, wrappers, bus timetables and Thermos flasks. And switch that phone off.

Advantages of field studies

It takes something special to persuade psychologists out of their laboratories to do their research. The main incentive for going out into the field can be summed up in three words – **good ecological validity**. Field studies enable researchers to study *everyday behaviour in everyday settings*. They're the ideal response to anyone who says psychologists draw their findings from giving people artificial tasks to do in artificial settings. See Chapter 2 for a longer discussion of *ecological validity*.

Because so many field studies are done covertly, you tend to get **no demand characteristics** (the section on controlled experiments has more about this). Participants who don't know they're in a study won't try to 'make it work out' the way the researcher wants it to. Nor will they try to 'spoil' the study for the researcher, so its outcome frustrates expectations. Reducing the effects of *demand characteristics* is really another consequence of allowing participants to behave 'naturally', the way they usually behave when no one's watching them.

Disadvantages of field studies

Some who favour a *qualitative* approach to doing research object to the use of **systematic observation** techniques in field studies. They say that if you focus on *prescribed behaviours* and record *these and these alone*, you miss the full richness and variety of your participants' behaviour. This is an example of *reductionism* (see Chapter 2 for more on this). You're also unable to take account of any unexpected behaviour that arises, if it falls outside the limits of your *prescribed behaviour*. In other words, *systematic observation* makes researchers too limited, too inflexible in what they observe.

The problem with working in the field is that **extraneous variables** are hard to control. Temperature, noise and many other variables are less predictable once you're outside the laboratory. With field *experiments* (as opposed to field observations) this lack of predictability is a particular drawback, since with this method you're trying to control any extraneous variables that might vary between your conditions. But the truth is that whatever variety of field study you're doing, you're only ever a moment away from complete disruption. Blizzards, dogs and marching bands can confound even the most carefully designed study. Could this be why most research is done under controlled conditions?

Method 5   Content analysis

A good private detective can find out a lot about someone simply by snooping around their living room, even when the subject of their investigations is dead, missing or on the other side of town. Once inside the living room, your private eye may well focus on two sources of information. First, she'll look at the books, videos and CDs that are lying around. Second, she'll look out for any scribbled notes, diaries, drawings or letters that carry the subject's signature. In short, she'll sift through the media messages the subject is exposed to (you could call these 'incoming messages') and the messages the subject has produced ('outgoing messages'). Messages like these will help the intrepid investigator build up a useful profile of the subject's tastes, motivations, desires, problems, heartaches, and so on.

Content analysis resembles this sort of detective work. It's a way of studying people *indirectly*, by analysing messages they expose themselves to and messages they produce – the television and films they watch; the books and newspapers they read; their letters, diaries, drawings and graffiti. Researchers who use this method reckon that *analysing* the *content* of messages helps us understand more about people's behaviour. For example, analysing what's in the cartoons we watch could tell us something about how violent we are in the playground, at work, at home. Or analysing the content of our newspapers might tell us something about how we voted in the last election.

How do you define content analysis?

It is defined as **a technique for assessing what's going on in messages**.

*Is content analysis **quantitative** or **qualitative**?*

You can do it either way. But for students who are just beginning their careers as researchers, the **quantitative** method tends to be favourite, so you'll find more space devoted to that approach in this section. Nevertheless, here are some details about the **qualitative** approach.

Qualitative content analysis is usually done by trained coders or 'content analysts'. This method, sometimes called 'semiology', involves *interpreting* **what's contained within messages in the light of what's known about its sender and its recipient**. In other words, you're looking at the *context* that the sender and recipient of a message are working in. This means taking notice of who's talking, as well as just what's being said. **Qualitative content analysis** might, for example, involve studying the use of 'persuasive cummunication' between two people having a conversation outside a bar. Or it might involve scouring television news coverage for examples of 'political bias'.

When you use this *interpretive* approach to content analysis you see the messages you're studying as being 'constructed' as part of an interaction between a giver and a receiver. They're not just messages studied in a vacuum, they're part of a conversation (or **discourse**, to use the parlance of semiologists). And of course because this method is so *interpretive*, different researchers are likely to analyse the content of the same messages in different ways.

In 1980 Bruner and Kelso published a study of 30 years of graffiti in public toilets (research cited in Bell et al., 1996). The content of these scrawlings was analysed qualitatively, for example in terms of gender differences. Female graffitists were reported as adopting a more inter-personal style, posing questions about relationships. Males took a more egocentric, confrontational approach to their art.

On the other hand, when you're doing **quantitative content analysis**, the emphasis is on studying *the message itself*. Rather than studying the people who produce and receive messages, the focus is on what's in the messages on their televisions, in their diaries, newspapers, on their videos, in their books, letters, e-mails, and so on.

In fact, when you do **quantitative content analysis** your first job is to select your **source material**. That's **what you're going to** *analyse* **the** *content* **of**. You can select more or less anything, so long as it's *some form of material that contains messages*. This gives you a pretty big choice – so big, in fact, that I'd be a fool to try and give you a definitive list of *possible sources*. Instead, here's a continuation of the list that appears in the previous paragraph: radio news, magazines, graffiti, movies, advertisements, children's drawings and stories, security videos, etc.

Once you've chosen your source material it's time to select a **target message**. In other words, **what you're going to focus on in your source material**. You can't analyse the entire content of your source material any more than you can observe everything your participants do in a field observation. So you need to *focus* on a specific message from your source material. Your choice of *possible target messages* is roughly as wide as the Grand Canyon, so again I'll avoid attempting to offer you a definitive list. Here's one idea, borrowed from some A-level students I worked with.

Gilbert and George (names fictitious) chose a series of Postman Pat *story books as their source material. For their target message they focused on how many characters were shown driving vehicles in the stories. They wanted to see if there were more male or female drivers in Greendale (the village Pat calls home). The aim of their study was to find out whether children's books portray males and females in stereotypical gender roles.*

Doing quantitative content analyses effectively

This involves stepping between a series of concealed traps and potholes. Here are a few of them, plus some suggested routes between them.

The 'no system' trap   Yes, this is the same trap that appears on the road to doing non-participant field observations, so you can turn back to the section on field studies for more on this. The key point here is to focus on a target message that's *easy to recognise, easy to define* and therefore easy to record numerically.

The 'lone analyst' trap   Again, a throwback to the section on non-participant field observations. Remember, using more than one researcher means you can be more confident about the reliability of your data.

The 'Itchy and Scratchy' trap Imagine you want to find out how much violence there is in an episode of *The Simpsons*, yet you restrict your content analysis to the bit with *Itchy and Scratchy* in it. (For non-Simpsons-literate readers, the violence level in the *Itchy and Scratchy* bit of *The Simpsons* is unrepresentative of the violence level in the show as a whole.) What's the problem with your study? You've selected a section of source material that's unrepresentative of the whole thing. Avoid this trap by analysing a healthy slab of material, whatever it is. Rather than using a few pages of a children's story, use *a series* of stories, like Gilbert and George did.

The 'no comparison' trap If Gilbert and George had *just* counted how many male drivers were careering around Greendale, this study would have lacked something. Instead, they *compared* the number of male and female drivers. Analysing two elements from your target message means you can make comparisons between them. Analysing only one element often produces research that has an empty feel about it.

Advantages of content analysis

Doing content analysis allows you a high degree of **control** over your research. Because you're analysing messages that people produce (outgoing) or expose themselves to (incoming), rather than actual behaviour of participants *at the time that it occurs*, you're spared the unpredictability of the 'live' research situation. Once you've got hold of your source material you can analyse it when and where you want.

When you do content analyses your **choice of source material** is, to put it mildly, extensive. Researchers are drawn to this method because it enables them to study more or less any kind of message they choose. In the case of 'incoming messages' – media output – the amount of material that's available for study is huge. And it's getting bigger.

Disadvantages of content analysis

Coolican (1996) describes quantitative content analysis as a method for 'reducing qualitative data' to a numerical form. Researchers who take a *qualitative* approach to research say that if you focus on a specific *target message* in your source material, then just *count how often it appears*, you're bound to miss a lot of what's going on in the material. They say you're being **reductionist**, that you're reducing a complex set of messages to an oversimplified form (see Chapter 2 for more on *reductionism*). Researchers who take this view prefer to carry out qualitative content analyses.

Doing content analysis is about studying messages, rather than the people who receive or produce them. So you could say it's a rather **indirect** form of research. Arguably, psychological research should focus on the person, not the message. We should study how people *respond* to incoming messages, like the books they read. We should try to find out how people *produce* outgoing messages, like pictures or stories. In short, we should be more direct.

Method 6   Correlational studies

Every summer when the men down our street discard their long trousers and start wearing shorts, ice-cream sales go sky high. Also, the rise of the mutliplex cinema in this area has been accompanied by an escalation in joyriding. In fact, our town is full of relationships like these – relationships between *pairs of variables* that appear to 'vary together', or **correlate**, as most psychologists would prefer to put it. Researchers use this term when they discuss variables that occur in 'real life'. Sometimes these are called **naturally occurring** variables, since they are **neither manipulated nor controlled by researchers**, in contrast to the *controlled* variables that *are* manipulated in laboratory experiments.

To say that a pair of variables **correlate** means they **alter their value at the same time as each other**. This can happen in two different ways. Firstly, as one goes up (or down), so does the other one. They follow each other, like a window cleaner and his shadow. Correlations like these, where **an increase (or decrease) in the value of one variable is accompanied by an increase (or decrease) in the value of the other**, are called **positive correlations**. For example, *an increase in* multiplex cinemas is accompanied by an *increase* in joyriding.

The other kind of correlation is called **negative correlation**. Here, **an increase (or decrease) in the value of one variable is accompanied by a decrease (or increase) in the value of the other**, like the two ends of a seesaw. Sometimes this is called *inverse* correlation. For example, the *fewer* men in long trousers, the *more* people buying ice creams.

So how would you define a correlational study?

It's **where researchers select a pair of naturally occuring variables, then measure the degree to which they vary at the same time as each other**. Your first job when you're planning to do a correlational study is to choose a pair of variables. Remember, you're looking for *naturally occurring*, 'real life' variables. What you're investigating is the kind relationship that exists between two variables that would be at large in the world (and going up and down) anyway, *whether or not you were studying them*. Examples of naturally occurring variables are climatic changes, crime figures, library attendances, college enrolments, ice-cream sales, dog immigration figures, and so on.

Zimbardo (1988) cites figures from the California Department of Education, correlating a pair of vairables: average hours of television watched daily by a group of schoolchildren and their performance in school reading tests. A negative correlation was found: the more television watched, the poorer the performance in reading tests.

*Are correlational studies **quantitative** or **qualitative**?*

Another look at our definition of correlational studies should clear this up. The word *measure* gives it away. Correlating a pair of variables involves assigning a *quantitative value* (a number) to the relationship between a pair of variables. So instead of saying that the rise of the multiplex cinema positively correlates with an increase in joyriding *'a lot'*, the results of a correlational study allow you to say that these variables have a correlation of a particular numerical value. It's this numerical precision that draws many researchers to this method.

The numerical value assigned to a pair of variables in a correlational study is called a **correlation co-efficient**. This is **a number measuring the degree to which a pair of variables are correlated**. It's always a number between −1 and +1. The closer it is to −1, the more negatively correlated a pair of variables is. The closer it is to +1, the more positively correlated they are. A co-efficient of zero shows 'no correlation'. **Box 3C** gives a summary of some of this information.

So how do you work out the correlation co-efficient for a pair of variables?

Once you've established which pair of variables you're going to use, calculating their correlation co-efficient involves using a set of fairly straightforward statistical procedures that feature in Chapter 4. The

Box 3C   Correlation co-efficients are numbers that fall between −1 and +1

                  A B   **C D E**   **F**   **G**
Correlation co-efficients: −1 −0.8 −0.6 −0.4 −0.2 0 0.2 0.4 0.6 0.8 +1

The scale shows a number of correlation co-efficients of varying
strengths. Co-efficient **A** shows **perfect negative correlation**, where
a pair of values move up and down together, like a window cleaner and
his shadow. Co-efficient **G** shows **perfect positive correlation**, like
the ends of a seesaw. 'Perfect correlations' such as these are rare in real
life. **F** and **B** show strongly positive (**F**) and negative (**B**) correlations. **C**
and **E** show weak correlations. Co-efficient **D** shows a relationship with
no correlation, where **variables in a pair alter their values independently of one another**, as in the relationship between egg
consumption and lepidopterology (moth collecting).

section on **inferential statistics** in Chapter 4 has a guide to *calculating correlation co-efficients*.

Doing correlational studies effectively
This involves treading lightly around and between a few notable trap-
doors. Here are some of the more dangerous ones, with suggestions
on how to steer clear of them.

   The 'unoperational variable' trap   Psychologists have pilfered
the idea of correlation from mathematicians. Doing correlational
studies really boils down to *assigning a mathematical value to the relationship between a pair of variables*. Given its quantitative nature, you
shouldn't be too shocked to discover that the key to doing effective
correlational research is selecting *quantifiable* variables. This means
ensuring the pair of variables you're correlating are **variables that
can be observed and measured**. Sometimes these are called
operational variables. Good examples of *naturally occurring operational* variables are 'temperature', 'unemployment', 'ice-cream sales'.
Bad examples are 'morale' and 'happiness', unless, of course, you
know of any effective ways of measuring these elusive qualities.

   The 'correlation and cause are two different things' trap
Although 'men wearing shorts' and 'ice-cream sales' are positively correlated, it would be foolish to assume that one *causes* the other. Both

these variables owe their fluctuations to a third variable – summer. It is a mistake to assign cause-and-effect relationships to variables that are correlated.

Correlation and cause are two different things. *Even where cause-and-effect relationships do exist, it's beyond the scope of correlational studies to uncover them.* This is because this method doesn't involve the strict controls that are necessary to even *contemplate* the establishment of cause-and-effect links. Correlation shows an *association* or *coincidence* between pairs of variables, that's all. Chapter 1 has a lengthy discussion of the uses and misuses of the word 'cause' in psychology.

The 'no means no' trap   It's silly, I know, but people who aren't fully concentrating on what they're doing sometimes get 'no correlation' mixed up with 'negative correlation' – probably because of their negative connotations. Just to be sure this never happens to you, look again at the definitions of the two. They're quite different, I think you'll agree.

Advantages of correlational studies

Correlational studies involve neither the manipulation nor the control of environmental variables. This is advantageous on two counts. One is that because you're using naturally occurring variables, your study will have a high degree of **ecological validity**. The other advantage of not manipulating the environment is that your study is likely to be **ethically sound**. Specifically, issues relating to participants' safety, their right to withdraw and debriefing don't arise at all in correlational research (see later in this chapter for a full review of ethical issues in research).

What draws many researchers to this method is the mathematical tool of correlation itself. Using co-efficients to measure relationships between pairs of variables means you can claim a high degree of **empiricism** for what you're doing. It means you can point to *observable, measurable associations* between variables to support your theories, rather than simply supporting them with unsubstantiated observations, ideas and anecdotes (Chapter 1 has a discussion of empiricism).

Disadvantages of correlational studies

The criticism on everybody's lips when it comes to correlational research is its **inability to establish cause-and-effect links**.

Researchers who favour more controlled methods, such as laboratory experiments, claim they *can* establish causal links, though even this is open to dispute (the section on 'causing' in **Chapter 1** covers this debate). Still, it's widely accepted that correlational research hasn't a hope of establishing causal links – only coincidences – between pairs of variables.

Findings from correlational studies measure how groups of people behave, yet **they tell us little about any given individual's behaviour**. It might be beneficial to know that *as a male*, you're likely to behave in a certain way as the temperature rises in the summer, *because you're part of the male population*. But findings like these tell us nothing about the individual motivations of particular male participants. You could say correlational studies treat people 'in herds'.

Method 7 Diary studies

Leafing through someone's diary is every psychologist's fantasy. If you want to know what someone's been up to, could there be a more reliable source than their own personal record – straight from the horse's mouth?

A diary can be an honest, even intimate account of what's going on in someone's life. True, you can find out plenty about a person by observing their behaviour or reading their responses to a questionnaire, but neither of these methods produces *first-hand tales, told in the participant's own words*.

Most people have had a go at keeping a diary. The popular technique is to compile a general, 'Captain's log' style résumé of the important events of the day. And who decides which events are important? Well, you, the diarist, do. And herein lies a key difference between traditional diaries and the diaries psychological researchers use. In research, it's *the researcher* who decides which topics are covered in that day's entries, not the diarist.

At the beginning of a diary study the diarist – or participant – is given what's called a **target variable**. This is **the aspect of the participant's life the researcher is interested in**. From then on the diarist is expected to keep a 'single-track minded' record of their behaviour relating to that variable.

For example, in a study by de Castro and de Castro (1989) participants were asked to record all their food-related behaviour for a week. Food-related behaviour was the target variable. They wrote down descriptions of their meals, where they ate, who they ate with and so on. They observed a strong relationship between ' meal size' and the number of people who were present whilst it was being eaten.

There's another striking difference between traditional diaries and the ones used in research. They look very different. Rather than the slim, personalised little volumes we so often get for Christmas, a research diary usually takes the form of a standardised set of response sheets with spaces for participants to fill in each day, hour, afternoon or whatever 'time interval' is being used. As well as having 'open-ended' spaces, these sheets often have standard questions to be answered each time the diary is filled in.

So how would you define a diary study?

Often called 'self-report', it's **a study where you ask participants to keep a personal record of their behaviour relating to a variable over a specified time period**.

*Are diary studies **qualitative** or **quantitative**?*

They tend to combine both. Typical diary studies have participants making *descriptive* entries in their diaries. They would write in detail about their behaviour relating to the target variable. This descriptive element makes it a *qualitative* study. Yet *quantitative* elements also play a part. For example, you might ask participants to record the number of times a particular behaviour occurs, or to record (say on a scale of 1 to 7, a so-called Likert scale) how strongly they feel about an event or behaviour. In one study, diarists were asked to rate how comfortable they felt in their working environment (Williamson and Barrow, 1994).

What happens to the diaries once they're complete?

When the diaries have been compiled and returned to you, you can set about analysing their content.

Analysing their content? That sounds familiar.

So it should. At this point a diary study really becomes an exercise in *content analysis* (see earlier in this chapter for a full description of this).

Your job as researcher is now to summarise or make sense of your participant's diary entries. How you do this depends on what your *target variable* is.

One way of analysing your data is to pick out the most common *categories* of behaviour, thoughts or feelings that feature in the diaries. For instance, if you were studying *eating habits* you might want to pick out what your participants have recorded as the most important features of a desirable eating environment. This would be a descriptive, *qualitative* exercise. You may also want to take *quantitative* measures. For instance, you might be interested in the average number of people present at each meal or how long the average meal takes to eat.

Doing diary studies effectively

This involves sidestepping several treacherous traps. Here are some of the most dangerous, plus some ideas on how to avoid them.

The 'no system' trap This one's common to *diary studies, content analysis* and *field studies*. Backtrack to the section on field studies for a full explanation. The key here is to limit your research to a *target variable* that's *easy to define, easy to recognise* and therefore easy to record numerically.

The 'gagging' trap Doing effective diary research means striking a balance between freedom of expression and 'gagging'. Allowing participants freedom to write what they want about a *target variable* may yield a stack of (albeit interesting) diaries that are difficult to analyse because they're written in a multitude of individual styles. On the other hand, if diarists are *prevented* from expressing themselves they'll be well and truly 'gagged'. Their diaries will be nothing more than standardised (questionnaire style) response sheets that prevent them from telling *first-hand tales in their own words*. So strike a balance. Design response sheets that incorporate *some* room for standardised responses on the target variable and *some* room for 'open-ended' reflections. Remember, one aim of diary research is to let participants tell their tales *in their own words*. So take care to preserve your diarists' own wording when recording *qualitative data* in your *research report*.

The 'great expectations' trap However big their hearts are, your diarists won't care about your research as much as you do. Yes, most of them will be happy to fill out their diaries each day but don't expect them to, say, give up all their afternoons. Ask yourself how long your response sheets take to complete. Then ask yourself how much time you can realistically ask of your participants. Be realistic. Half an hour a day is a lot to ask – ten minutes is nearer the mark. It's a good idea to include, on your response sheets, a clear recommendation about how much to write each day.

The 'disappearing diarists' trap   Diary research can come to a sorry end when researchers lose touch with diarists in mid-study. Response sheets are duly delivered to participants with clear instructions about what's expected of them – and that's the last you see of either of them. A disappearing diarist (or 'participant attrition' as researchers like to call it) is bound to happen occasionally. But there are steps you can take to minimise it. Above all, make sure diarists have *clear written instructions*: about what to write about, about when and how to return the diaries when the deed is done, about how to contact you with any queries and so on. Also, it's a good idea for you to contact each diarist once the study is under way, just to remind them that you're interested in what they're up to.

Advantages of diary studies

Diary studies **raise the participants' profile** in psychological research. So many methods reduce participants to the level of 'objects to be studied' (controlled experiments, field studies), whose own voices are rarely heard in the research. In diary studies participants' voices come through loud and clear. They retain some control over what is reported and the style of reporting that's used. After all, in self-report research participants are reporting on themselves, rather than being reported on by others.

Self-report diaries give you access to **relatively private behaviours that are unobservable in the field or in the laboratory**. They give you a 'backstage pass' into the lives of your participants. This means you can develop an interest in aspects of behaviour that are normally kept fairly private – such as diet, health, hygiene and leisure. Using a self-report method has the added advantage of allowing you to study your participants in a fairly detailed way without resorting to deception.

Disadvantages of diary studies

Since self-report research relies on the participants taking control of data collection, it's bound to yield **unverifiable data**. Checking how truthful or accurate diarists have been with their entries is, of course, out of the question. No second opinion is available. Perhaps this explains why diary studies remain outside the mainstream of psychological research.

Once the response sheets have been returned to you, diary studies really become an exercise in content analysis. Your job is to summarise and make sense of what's been written. As with content analysis, this process of 'summarising and making sense' of text can all too easily descend into **reductionism**. In other words, you may find yourself reducing the complexities of the diary entries to soundbites (see Chapter 2 for more on *reductionism*).

Before leaving this section, let's eavesdrop on a group of (fictitious) A-level psychology students to find out what they have to say in response to the question: *Why do you think these methods are so popular and practical for doing research on undergraduate psychology courses?* **Box 3D** has their answers.

Now you have some idea about *how* you're going to do your study, it's time you turned your thoughts to *who* you're going to study.

▶ Skill no. 3: Selecting your participants

Unless you're doing a content analysis (in which case you won't need any participants) or a case study (where you'll need precious few) your next job is to find a **sample** of participants to study. Whether you're planning a *controlled experiment*, a *questionnaire* or a *field study*, you'll need to consider *who* your participants are going to be and *how* you're going to get hold of them.

One thing's certain: you can't study everyone. It would take too long. Instead, you need to find yourself a *select group* of participants to take part in your research. This *select group* will be your **sample**. The art of selecting them is called **sampling**.

How about going out and picking the first 20 people I bump into?

You could do that. But it's risky. The first 20 people you bump into will probably include *quite a few* representatives from some groups in society and *hardly any* representatives from others. You might bump into 15 men and only five women. Or 20 people without disabilities. Or 20 hunter-gatherers. Or a marching band. So you might end up with **a group of participants that overrepresents some groups in the population and underrepresents others**. This is what researchers

Box 3D Why are these methods so popular and practical?

A popular, practical method is . . .	'I think it's popular and practical because . . .
Controlled experiment	. . . it enables you to do your study "all in one go". Once you've found yourself a room to use as a "laboratory" and gathered together your participants, the whole study can be done in an afternoon.'
Case study	. . . you only need one or two participants. So although you're gathering detailed data, you don't need to spend time finding lots of participants.'
Questionnaire	. . . once you've constructed your questionnaire it's a fairly straightforward task to collate your results. Also, using questionnaires means you can combine the quantitative and qualitative approaches.'
Field study	. . . it enables you to do your study in the real world, like in a shopping mall or in the street. This means that as long as you don't inconvenience anyone, you can do your study "undercover".'
Content analysis	. . . you find out a lot about TV programmes, magazines or whatever it is you're studying. You can look "behind the headlines" and "in between the lines" of what journalists and programme makers are really saying.'
Correlational study	. . . you can draw links between variables that move up and down together and you can measure the size of the link. Plus, you don't actually have to assemble any participants. You can use crime figures and suchlike.'
Diary study	. . . you get to hear how participants describe what they're doing and how they feel about it. You can hear their way of putting it. It's more personal, somehow.'

call an **unrepresentative sample**. It's your job to find a way of stopping yourself from selecting this kind of sample.

In this section I'm going to suggest *four ways of stopping yourself from selecting an unrepresentative sample* for your research. First though, there are three groups of people I really must introduce you to. No doubt you yourself are a member of at least one of these groups.

Samples, sampling populations and populations

Introducing *Group A*, **the sample**. These are **the participants you'll study in your research**.

Introducing *Group B*, **the sampling population**. These are the people who are *in danger* of being selected as participants for your research. This is **the group who you'll draw your sample from**. If you're doing your study at a university, you're drawing your sample from a sampling population of 'university students'. If you're doing your study at a leisure centre, your sampling population is 'leisure centre users'.

Introducing *Group C*, **the population**. This is **the group who the results of your study will apply to**. If you're doing a study about problem solving amongst university students, you'll no doubt want to apply your results to a population of 'all normal problem-solving adults'. If you're doing a study about courtship and flirting behaviour amongst leisure centre users, you'll probably go on to apply your results to a population of 'normal adults'.

Now stop. Look again at *Groups B* and *C*. They're not quite the same, are they? *Group B* is smaller than *Group C*. **Psychology's best-kept secret** is that *researchers regularly draw their samples from a particular, restricted sampling population*, namely, 'university undergraduates'. Then they go on to apply their results to a *population* of 'all normal adults'. You could say they're shooting themselves in the foot by doing this, since they're bound to end up doing their research on unrepresentative samples of participants. So why do they do it? They do it because psychological research takes place in universities and universities are teeming with undergraduates. They're widely available. For this reason some critics of psychology have mischievously altered its name from *the study of human behaviour and experience* to *the study of undergraduate behaviour and experience*.

Four ways to select a representative sample

Having exposed psychology's best kept secret, let's get back to the business of selecting a sample of participants that neither underrepresents, nor overrepresents, any particular social group. Here are four popular sampling methods.

Method 1: Simple random sampling. When you use this method **everyone in your sampling population has an equal chance of being selected** as a participant for your study. Note that this isn't the same as saying that everyone in the *population* has an equal chance of being selected. Populations are bigger than sampling populations, remember. However, the bigger your *sampling population* is, the more representative of the *population* as a whole your sample will be. Here are some techniques of doing random sampling:

- **The 'college roll' technique** is useful if you're using your college as your sampling population. It's a bit restricted, but very convenient. Simply give everyone on the roll a number, then select a random sample of numbers. Most spreadsheet or statistics software packages incorporate a *random number generator*. You'll find a *random number table* in Appendix 2. Alternatively, do it manually. Have all the names from the roll on bits of paper and pick a sample of them out of a hat. This technique works well for controlled experiments.

- **The 'electoral roll' technique** is useful if you're looking for a sampling population that covers your community, rather than just your college. Virtually every adult is on the electoral roll (this isn't true of, say, your local phone book, which omits non-phone-owners). Once you've got hold of a copy of the electoral roll for your area, use any of the methods I suggested in the previous paragraph for selecting your random sample (although this method's a bit beyond the scope of the 'names out of a hat' method). This technique works well for questionnaire studies.

Method 2: Stratified random sampling. This method is similar to simple random sampling, with an additional, preliminary phase. Before selecting your sample you do a little detective work on your sampling population. You find out its proportions, according to certain variables that you think are relevant to your study. For example, if you're doing a gender-related study you might take the trouble to find out that 50 per cent of your sampling population are male, 50 per cent female. Or if you're doing a health-related study you might take the trouble to find out that 30 per cent of your sampling population are smokers, 70 per cent non-smokers.

Following this preliminary, 'detective' stage, you go on to select your participants, taking care to **reproduce, in your sample, the proportions that exist in your sampling population**. So let's say you want a sample of 50 participants. In the case of the gender-related study you'd separate your sampling population into males and females, then randomly choose 25 of each (using any of the methods I suggested in the simple random sampling section). For the health-related study you'd randomly select 35 participants from the non-smoking contingent and 15 from the smoking contingent.

Stratified random sampling works well with any method, so long as you're able to find out the proportions that make up your sampling population. True, it requires some extra detective work. But this helps you to make sure that certain groups that are relevant to your study are fairly represented in your sample.

Method 3:   Systematic random sampling. Again, this method is 'simple random sampling with a difference'. Instead of selecting your sample from your sampling population by using some form of *random number generation*, you do it by nominating a *system* by which you **select every fifth, tenth (or whatever number you prefer) member of your sample population** until you have enough participants for your study. For instance, you might select every tenth name on your college roll, every 17th person who walks down a corridor. You might even call at every third house in your street. This method works well with research that takes place in the field, though it's a fair method for using with questionnaires and controlled experiments, too.

Method 4:   Quota sampling. If you don't have any details about the proportions that make up your sampling population (for example, if you haven't had time to do the necessary detective work) **quota sampling** could be for you. As with stratified random sampling, the aim here is to **reproduce, in your sample, the proportions that exist in your sampling population**. But unlike stratified random sampling, you do it **without knowing the proportions that exist in your sampling population**.

Hang on. How can you reproduce the proportions of something you don't know the proportions of?

Easy – guesswork. Make an informed *guess*. Again, let's say you're looking for a sample of 50 participants. In the case of gender you can make an informed *guess* that 50 per cent of your sampling population are female, 50 per cent male. Then, when you've done your guessing, you go ahead and find yourself 25 males and 25 females to do your research on. These are your *quotas*. Or in the case of smoking you can make an informed *guess* that 30 per cent of your sampling population smoke, 70 per cent don't. Then you go ahead and select quotas of 35 non-smokers and 15 smokers.

So quota sampling is based on 'informed guesswork' rather than 'detective work', right?

Right. And it's different from stratified random sampling in another way, too. Once you've decided (guessed) how many representatives you want from each group, instead of selecting them *randomly* you go out and pick the first, say, 25 males you come across, or the first 25 females. You could say that, once you've decided on the size of your quotas, all you're doing is choosing the first 25 people you bump into.

Quota sampling is popular with market researchers. When they ignore you in shopping malls and ask someone else how often they use *Polyfilla*, it may be because they've filled their quota of 'people like you', not because they don't like the look of you. It works well with face-to-face questionnaire studies and field experiments, too.

Now let's do some more eavesdropping, this time on a group of (imaginary) first-year undergraduate psychology students who are discussing the merits and demerits of the different sampling methods (see **Box 3E**).

Now you've chosen your sample, it's time think about how to treat them *ethically* during your research.

▶ Skill no. 4: Treating your participants ethically

Post-traumatic stress disorder (PTSD) affects people who've been exposed to distressing incidents. Fires and floods are typical examples. People who experience PTSD find it hard to expel the incident from their thoughts; they have bad dreams and flashbacks. In a word, they're 'traumatised'. In 1980 American psychiatrists included PTSD in their directory of psychiatric disorders' – the *Diagnostic Statistical Manual* (DSM) – for the first time (see American Psychiatric Association, 1980). Inclusion in the DSM made PTSD a properly recognised mental illness. People had always suffered from it, but now it was official.

Box 3E What are the merits and demerits of the different sampling methods?

	'One of its merits is ...	'One of its demerits is ...
Simple random sampling	... its "randomness". Everyone in your sampling population has an equal chance of being picked.'	... you can get an unrepresentative sample because you don't take into account the proportions in the sampling population.'
Stratified random sampling	... that in relation to a variable like gender you can make the proportions in your sample the same as those in your sampling population.'	... that you can only use it if you know all about the make-up of your sampling population.'
Systematic random sampling	... it stops you choosing people whom you like the look of and avoiding people whom you don't like the look of. You have to follow your system.'	... it could produce unrepresentative samples. If you chose every tenth house on a street and they were all even numbers, they might all be on the posh side.'
Quota sampling	... you don't need to know the make-up of your sampling population and you still get a pretty representative sample.'	... it's a bit unreliable because you have to guess the proportions of your sampling population. You might guess wrong.'

PTSD isn't like other psychiatric disorders. It has a different legal status from all the other 549 conditions in the DSM. Unlike depression, schizophrenia and the rest, legally speaking you can trace the onset of PTSD back to a specific incident. This means you can blame its onset on whoever was responsible for exposing you to the incident, *then* try to claim compensation. Employees regularly sue employers on these grounds. Some day someone will blame *their* bad dreams or flashbacks on an incident they were exposed to not by an employer, but by a psychological researcher whilst participating in one of their studies. A lengthy legal wrangle will ensue.

To make sure your research doesn't end this way, observe the ***Eight guidelines for treating human participants ethically*** outlined below as you do your study.

Guideline 1

When you're writing your *research report* avoid mentioning your participants' names. They'll be happier to take part in your research (and for you to write about what they did) if you guarantee them, *before your study starts*, that you'll respect their **anonymity**. Tell your participants: *'Rest assured, your names won't be used when we write our research reports.'*

Guideline 2

If you're doing overt research (where participants know they're being studied) inform your participants what the study involves and about any inconvenience they're likely to suffer. Do this *before your study starts*. If they know what they're letting themselves in for they can give you their **informed consent**. However, there may be some things you don't want to divulge, since doing so might lead your participants to behave unnaturally. In cases like this, let your participants know they're not being told everything. This gives them the option to withdraw. If your participants are children, consent has to be obtained from whoever's responsible for them. Tell your participants: *'Since the aims of our study require you to behave naturally, we're keeping some of its procedures secret. But rest assured, you're in no danger. However, if you're concerned about not being fully informed, feel free to withdraw at any stage.'*

Guideline 3

Most psychological researchers conceal some details about their research from their participants. Some degree of **deception** is commonplace, especially where it's reasonable to assume that complete openness might lead to unnatural behaviour. But how far should you go? How do you decide how much deception to employ? To help answer these questions there are two groups of people you can consult *before your study begins*: first, people of a similar age and background to your participants: second, your own fellow researchers. Ask people from both groups if *they* think you're deceiving your participants in a way that could cause them anxiety if they were to find out about it at a future date. If they say you're overstepping the mark, alter your design. Ask your colleagues: *'Here's an outline of what we intend to do in our research. If you were a participant in this study, would you be anxious about the level of deception involved?'*

Guideline 4

Leave participants as you found them, is the message here. Do this by giving them a thorough **debriefing** *after your study is done.* Try to ensure that anyone who takes part in your study feels as comfortable with themselves (and with psychological research) as they did beforehand. All experiences affect us in some way, so they won't feel *exactly the same* as they did before taking part. But by explaining the true aims of your study and thanking them for their co-operation, you can ensure that your participants don't walk away with bad memories, muttering to themselves about how they'll never take part in psychological research again. Tell your participants: *'Thanks for your time and co-operation. If you'd like to know more about the true aims of our study I'll be happy to go over them with you. If you'd like a copy of our research report, remember to leave us your e-mail address before you leave. Do take a biscuit on your way out.'*

Guideline 5

The politeness of some participants is such that even if they're experiencing pain and distress during your study, they won't say anything, not wanting to rock the boat. Suffering in silence like this is clearly of benefit to no one. You can't prevent it altogether, but you can make it less likely. *Before your study begins*, explain clearly to your participants that they have the **right to withdraw** *at any stage.* And if, at any stage, *you* feel that your participants are experiencing pain and distress, close it down. Don't just grit your teeth and hang on until the end. Err on the side of caution. Tell your participants: *'As it says in our briefing document, if you begin to feel uneasy about anything that happens during our study you can withdraw at any stage. And if, after the study is finished, you'd prefer us not use the data relating to your behaviour, we'll be happy to withdraw and destroy them there and then.'*

Guideline 6

Be sure to inform your participants that anything you find out about them during your study will be treated with **confidentiality**. Assurances like these are especially important when you're dealing with responses to questionnaires about sensitive subjects (religion, sex, food, etc.). If, however, one of your participants commits a misdemeanour or felony (theft, violence, damage, etc.) during your study, you're within your rights to break this confidence. Tell your participants: *'As it says in our briefing document, you can rest assured that any information you provide during our study will be treated in confidence.'*

Guideline 7

A recent change in psychological terminology has seen researchers adopt the term 'participant', rather than 'subject', to refer to the members of their sample. This signals a change in attitude, too. Researchers are keener to see those who take part in their studies as having feelings and rights. The old 'it's all right to *subject* people and animals to physical and psychological discomfort, so long as it's in the interests of science' attitude is thankfully on the wane. **Protection of participants** is *de rigueur*. So it's up to you to protect *your* participants from any discomfort during your study. One way of showing your concern is to find out, *before your study begins*, if anyone taking part in your study has a medical condition that might put them at risk. Tell your participants: *'Rest assured, during our study you won't experience any more physical or mental stress than you would if you weren't taking part. Remember, you can raise the alarm if you do experience any discomfort at any stage. We'll be on hand if you need us. Also, if anyone has any of the medical conditions listed on our briefing document, please let us know before we start.'*

Guideline 8

Doing research involving **covert participation** means dealing with a peculiar set of circumstances. You can't obtain consent from your participants. Deception is inevitable. The right to withdraw is inapplicable. Debriefing is impractical. So how can you do a covert field study ethically? As a rule of thumb you should ensure that you don't study participants in situations where they aren't on public view *in any case*. And since most of these studies take place in public places like malls or cafés, you shouldn't have any problems there. If your study involves *intervening* in what your participant is doing (as in many *field experiments*) rather than just observing them (as in *field observations*) make sure you don't have them doing anything they wouldn't be likely to do in the normal course of events. Asking someone the time, or for assistance in crossing a road, is fine. Stealing their shopping isn't.

*What's a **briefing document***?

Treating participants with courtesy, gratitude and consideration makes sense twice over. First, they'll be more likely to behave naturally. Second, they'll be more likely to volunteer to take part in psychological research again. The last thing you want is a sample of seething, short-tempered participants, desperate for clear instructions about what they're meant to be doing and how long they're expected to hang around. Remember, these people don't *have* to take part in your study. So in the interests of keeping them well informed it's a good idea to present them with a **briefing document** *before your study begins*. The aim here is **to answer some of the questions participants typically ask** about what is, after all, an unusual situation for them. The scope of the document will vary according to the kind of study you're doing, but generally it will include:

- advice about medical conditions that might put them at risk if they take part in your study;
- assurances about anonymity, confidentiality and their right to withdraw;
- information about the level of deception in your study;
- information about the aims of your study, though you might not want to divulge all your aims;
- instructions about what they're expected to do during the study;
- your e-mail address, in case participants want a copy of your research report;
- Your gratitude for their time and effort.

Apart from making everyone feel more at ease, your briefing document saves you the bother of having to remember to make a series of announcements at the beginning of your study. It is much easier to have it all pre-prepared. Plus, it gives you 'an air of professionalism' that ought to make your participants take you and your research seriously.

If you treat your participants ethically the chances of them walking away from your study with bad memories of what you put them through will be slim. By 'treating people right' you can uphold the reputation of psychological researchers as a communicative, considerate, competent bunch who don't mean any harm. And as a representative of a bunch with a reputation like that, you ought to find willing participants for future studies easier to come by.

What about the ethics of doing research on animals?

Psychological research using non-humans has its own set of ethical guidelines. As I'm writing for students on undergraduate courses which – I assume – only use human participants, I'm skipping these guidelines here. If you want to know more about the ethics of doing research with non-humans *or* human participants, publications by the British Psychological Society – *Guidelines for the Use of Animals in Research* and *Ethical Principles for Conducting Research with Human and Non-human Participants* – should tell you all you need to know.

Let's conclude this section by eavesdropping on a group of (fictional) psychology Access students who are discussing ethical issues relating to three familiar studies. See **Box 3F**.

You've done your ethical research. Now it's time to encapsulate it in your *research report.*

▶ Skill no. 5: Writing your research report

However skilfully you design and execute your study, you'll gain most of your marks for the way you write it up. Writing **research reports** isn't like writing essays. True, there are similarities: you need a similar level of detail and the word limit is similar (around 2000 words on most undergraduate courses, though it varies). The big difference is, **research reports** follow a recommended format – a set of conventions for dividing them into predetermined sections. Although following the format isn't *compulsory*, it's *conventional* on most courses, so I'm going to stick to it here.

Before guiding you through the format, though, let me introduce you to the kind of pearl of wisdom that might easily fall out of a cracker at the British Psychological Society Christmas party:

Box 3F   Did these researchers treat their participants ethically?

Latane and Darley's laboratory experiment (1968)	'Not really. For one thing, they deceived them by not initially revealing the true aims of the study, though if they had the participants might not have acted naturally. For another thing, the smoke coming out of the wall might have been traumatic. Especially if there were any pyrophobics in the sample.' (See pp. 66–71 for an outline of this study.)
Bales's non-participant observation (1958)	'Unusually for a field study, Bales's participants knew they were being observed. So there was a minimum of deception. Also, they gave their consent to the researchers. There was nothing really harmful or potentially traumatic in this study. All in all, these participants were treated ethically. Though I wonder whether they behaved naturally, given that they knew Big Brother was watching.' (See p. 55 for an outline of this study.)
Middlemist et al.'s field experiment (1976)	'Definitely not. Being a typical field experiment, no consent was obtained. Although these toilets were public, it isn't really the kind of place you expect to be observed. It's in that public–private "neitherworld". What's more, it can be traumatic to crowd someone whilst they're trying to "go". Also, I bet there was no debriefing. Would you want to debrief someone after a study like that?' (See p. 83 for an outline of this study.)

Effective research reports should be written clearly enough for the reader to replicate the research without asking for any further clarifications.

If you say these words to yourself before you start writing your report, then again at regular intervals whilst you're writing it, your work will be better for it. The recommended format for a **2000-word** report is as follows.

Title

Your **title** shouldn't just tell your reader what your research is about. It should tell them which **variables** you're studying (see the section on controlled experiments in this chapter for a full discussion of *variables*). Thus *The relationship between gender and the criteria we use for making moral decisions* is a more informative title than, say, *An investigation into moral dilemmas*.

Abstract

Your **abstract** summarises your report. When you pick up a book in a shop you base your decision about whether or not to buy it on the *blurb* on the back. *Abstracts* have a similar function for *research reports*. They provide a *summary*, in around *150 words*, of the *aim* of your study, its *method*, the make-up of your *sample* and your *findings* (including, where appropriate, the outcome of any **inferential statistical tests** you've done – see Chapter 4 for more on these). After reading your *abstract* your reader should be able to make an informed decision about whether to bother reading your entire report. Although the *abstract* appears at the beginning of your report, some students prefer to write it last, since by then they're able to take a step back and summarise what they've done.

Introduction

Your **introduction** is the first 'long section' in your report – around *500 words*. An effective *introduction* does three jobs. It explains the **background** to your study, its **aims** and your **expectations** about its findings.

Explain the **background** to your study by giving your reader a round-up of the relevant psychological research into the area you're studying. It's the convention to move from the 'general to the particular'. In other words, set the scene first, then get to specifics. Start by introducing the *general* psychological concepts you're dealing with (and describe some theories or studies that relate to them), then introduce the *specific* concepts your research addresses (and again, describe some related studies and theories). An example of a *general* psychological concept is 'prejudice'. A *specific* concept would be 'prejudice towards particular racial groups in the USA' (see Lapiere's study, described in the section on *methods*, earlier in this chapter).

To explain the **aims** of your study, set out your *research rationale* (see *skill no. 1* earlier in this chapter for an explanation of these) and relate it to the research you described in the first part of your *intro-*

duction. Show how research by other psychologists leaves a 'gap in our understanding' that still needs to be filled. Your study is an attempt to fill this gap. *For example, the research background to Lapiere's study showed that there were prejudiced attitudes towards certain racial groups in the USA. From this Lapiere identified a gap in our understanding of the link between attitudes reflecting prejudice and behaviour reflecting prejudice.*

To explain your **expectations** about the outcome of your study, spell out your **hypothesis** (see the section on *proving* in Chapter 1 for a full discussion of hypotheses). This is the culmination of your *introduction*. You've written *generally* about the background to your study, now finish with a *specific prediction* about what you expect to find. An effective hypothesis is **operational**. This means it should **clearly state the variables that appear in your research**. An hypothesis like *There will be racial prejudice against Chinese people* is too vague. A clearer, more operational hypothesis for Lapiere's study would be *There will be a difference in hoteliers' responses to the request to serve Chinese people, depending on whether it is made in a face-to-face setting or on a questionnaire.*

If your reader is still in the dark about what your research is about and what you expect to find *after* reading your *introduction*, something has gone badly wrong.

Method

Your method *should be written clearly enough for the reader to replicate your research without asking for any further clarifications.* Here's where that pearl of wisdom from the Christmas cracker comes into its own. This is the 'instruction manual' section of your report. It's where your reader finds out how they can do your research for themselves. The *method* should be around *250 words* long. It's conventional to break it up into four sections:

- **The design** Here, set out the structure of your study. Describe what *method* you used, how many *conditions* you had and how you divided your participants into conditions. Did you use an *independent, repeated measures* or *matched pairs* design? Say also what your *independent* and *dependent variables* were. You should also explain what measures you used to control any *extraneous variables*. Did you, for example, use *counterbalancing*? (See the section on *controlled experiments* earlier in this chapter for a fuller discussion of all these design concepts.)

- **The sample** Explain *which* sections of the population you drew your participants from, *how many* of them were in each condition and *how* you selected them. Explain which *sampling method* you used. (See *skill no. 3* in this chapter for a round-up of these *sampling methods.*)

- **The materials** What equipment or props would a would-be researcher need to replicate your study? Either set this bit out as a list or as a short description, so long as it includes all the necessary items, such as *briefing documents* (see the section on *ethics*, earlier in this chapter, for more on these), stopwatches, questionnaires, word lists, whiteboards, calculators, hooters, bells, and so on.

- **The procedure** This is a concise, step-by-step account of how you did your study. As always, employ a written style that's explicit, unambiguous and uncluttered. Don't complicate your *procedure* with your feelings about how you think it went. Just say what you did. Include word-for-word transcriptions of any instructions you give to your participants. If you used a *questionnaire* don't forget to outline how you wrote it.

Results

Your results section sets out, in around *300 words*, what you found from your research. This word limit doesn't include tables or graphs. As for raw data and statistical calculations, save them for your *appendix*. It's conventional to divide this section into two parts. If you're doing *quantitative* research your report will only be complete if it has *parts 1 and 2*. If you're doing *qualitative* research, include *part 1* only:

- **Part 1: describing the results** Present your findings in a way that's easy to understand and easy on the eye. Start by outlining your main findings *in words*. Either use point form or clearly laid out paragraphs, whichever you're most comfortable with.

  If you're doing *qualitative* research illustrate your description with key observations or quotes from your participants. If you're doing *quantitative* research use key numerical findings to illustrate your description: for example, measures of **central tendency** (showing average scores) and **dispersion** (showing how well spread your scores are). Also, support your descriptions of *quantitative* findings with other **descriptive statistics** (Chapter 4 has a full discussion of these). This means using one or two charts, graphs or tables *where you feel they add to the clarity of your descriptions*. Present them attractively and label them so clearly that someone with a poor attention span, hardly any patience and no interest in psychology can make sense of them.

• **Part 2: analysing the results**   Here, deal with any **inferential statistical test** you used to support your findings (Chapter 4 has a detailed guide to using these). The aim of this bit of your report is to answer three questions for your reader. One, *which* **inferential test** did you use? Second, *why* did you select this **inferential test** in preference to all the others? Third, did the *outcome* of this **inferential test** give statistical support for your findings? The conventions involved in answering these and other important questions about **inferential tests** are dealt with in Chapter 4, so I won't dwell on them here.

Discussion

Your discussion is the second 'long section' in your report, around *500 words*. Your first 'long section', the *introduction*, moved from *generally* familiarising your reader with your research area to dealing with the *particulars* of your study. Your *discussion* does the reverse. Here you're going to restate what your *particular* study found, then relate it to the *general* research area. So your *research report* should have a kind of *zoom-in-zoom-out* feel to it.

Start by **restating your findings.** Say whether your hypothesis is *supported* or not (remember, hypotheses aren't *proved* or *disproved*, they're *supported* or *rejected* – see Chapter 1 for a detailed discussion of this).

Next, *relate what you've found to* **other researchers' findings.** Do your results support or challenge what other psychologists have found? Your aim here is to place your own research back into the context you plucked it from in your *introduction*. You've zoomed in, now you're zooming out. For instance, Middlemist et al. (see the section on *ethics* in this chapter for more on this study) might include the following statement in this part of their discussion: *The findings from our work in public conveniences are supported by a number of other studies that have looked at the effects of stress. An example of such a study is . . .*

Next, **evaluate your study** and *suggest how, if you did it again, you might alter its design.* As a guide to evaluating your research use

the DRREEEEEAAAMSS system (you'll find a detailed explanation of this Chapter 2). Although **DRREEEEEAAAMSS** is designed to help you pick out positive *and* negative features of research, when applying it to your *own* study, err on the *critical* side. Identify weaknesses in your research, then suggest some possible modifications to the design. Middlemist et al. might, for instance, say something like: *Although we did our observations in a 'public' toilet, you could say it was unethical because you don't normally expect to be observed in such a setting. If we repeat this study it might be better to observe the effect of stress on a truly public activity, such as giving directions or reading a newspaper.*

Finally, *suggest some* **uses for your research findings** *and some* **ideas for future studies** *into your chosen topic.* Your aim here is to convince your reader that your research contributes to psychology's grand project of 'promoting human welfare'. Middlemist et al. might argue that *Research of this kind has implications for education. Educationalists could benefit from understanding how putting people in stressful situations can adversely affect their performance. It could explain why some 'bright' students perform poorly in examinations.*

References

Your reference section should include all the books and articles you've referred to in your report. Chapter 2 has a guide to the conventions of referencing. Do follow them. You'll be docked, nailed and penalised if you don't.

Appendix

Your appendix section is a repository for all the bits and pieces you want your tutor, lecturer or examiner to see, though you feel they're too 'rough and ready' for the main body of your report. Include raw data, examples of questionnaires, transcriptions of broadcasts or interviews, instructions to researchers or participants, briefing documents (see the section on *ethics* in this chapter for a guide to these), stimulus materials, calculations from statistical tests, photographs – whatever you feel is necessary to supplement your report. Most importantly, be sure to label whatever you include and refer to it in your main report.

Let's end this section with a final bit of eavesdropping, this time on a hypothetical e-mail discussion between a group of psychology tutors (see **Box 3G**).

Box 3G   What are the most common mistakes in each section of a research report?

Title	'Being vague. In other words, not stating the variables that the research is dealing with.'
Abstract	'Forgetting to put the results in. An abstract is meant to include the results, plus the outcome of any statistical tests. Plenty of students miss this out.'
Introduction	'Missing the hypothesis off the end. This is a common error and it's such a shame because the hypothesis is meant to be what the introduction is leading up to. Would you tell a joke with no punch-line?'
Method	'Omitting important details out of the procedure, so that anyone wanting to do a replication wouldn't have a clue.'
Results	'Badly labelled graphs and tables. In other words, descriptive statistics that are only decipherable to the person that wrote the report.'
Discussion	'Overly hurried work. Since this is the last big section, students tend to fluff it by doing it in a hurry. They can see the end in sight, I suppose.'
References	'Leaving it out altogether. Which is peculiar, since it's simple to do and it does gain a couple of marks.'
Appendices	'Unlabelled data and questionnaires that aren't referred to in the main report.'

Now you've selected your *research rationale*, settled on a *method*, picked your *participants*, studied them *ethically* and all but written your *research report*, your study is just about done – unless you need help with your **descriptive** and **inferential statistics**, in which case you'll be needing Chapter 4.

▶ **The last word**

Psychological research may be the most unpredictable aspect of under-graduate psychology. Because you're dealing with fellow researchers, participants, equipment, the unpredictable world of 'the field', there are lot of circumstances that are hard to forsee.

Although Chapter 3 won't make your research experience any more predictable, it should help you negotiate some of its more 'difficult corners' with a handy set of skills, guidelines, rules of thumb and pearls of wisdom. Here's a reminder of some of them:

- select something you're interested in for your research topic;
- no method is superior to another. They all have advantages and disadvantages;
- when choosing participants, find a way of stopping yourself from selecting an unrepresentative sample;
- in the interests of keeping your participants well informed, it's a good idea to present them with a briefing document;
- effective research reports should be written clearly enough for the reader to replicate the research without asking for any further clarifications.

4 Skills for Using Statistics in Psychology

> To newcomers in psychology it isn't entirely obvious why there's any need to develop statistical skills in a social science that's meant to be about human behaviour. In fact, many psychologists who prefer to do qualitative research have very little to do with statistics. But as you'll have realised from reading Chapter 3, it's very common for psychologists to measure human behaviour quantitatively. And whenever behaviour is being measured like this, skills for using statistics are much needed.
>
> This chapter is a guide to how and why statistics are useful for studying psychology. It provides you with as many statistical skills as you'll need to prosper at undergraduate level. A calculating machine will be handy now and again. Expertise in mathematics will be surplus to requirements.

Not all psychologists use statistics. If you're doing *qualitative* research you might prefer to describe your findings in words – without graphs, without tables, without numbers. But wherever there's a *quantitative* aspect to your research you'll find some of the skills in this chapter useful. Chapter 3 has more on the difference between *qualitative* and *quantitative* research.

Imagine a pair of psychology undergraduates doing their research. Call them Terry and Geri. They've chosen their *research rationale,* settled on a *methodology*, picked their *participants*, studied them *ethically* and all but written their *research reports*. Their research is nearly done.

All that remains is for them to dabble in **two kinds of statistics** so that they can complete their study and put the finishing touches to their *research reports*. These **two kinds of statistics** have different uses. They look different on paper. They have different names. One's called **descriptive statistics**, the other **inferential statistics**. This chapter is a guide to their use.

*So what are these **two kinds of statistics**, and what are they for?*

I'll come to that presently. First, let's take a look at Terry and Geri's research:

Terry and Geri did a modified version of Latane and Darley's 1968 controlled experiment, which looked at participants' reactions to an emergency situation (Chapter 3 has a review of this study). As you may recall, half of Latane and Darley's participants were asked to fill in a questionnaire individually, whilst the other half completed theirs in a group situation. So the independent variable (IV) was 'other people'. Latane and Darley pumped steam (mimicking smoke) through a grille in a wall of the experimental room and recorded how long it took participants to raise the alarm. So the dependent variable (DV) was 'response time'.

*Terry and Geri modified Latane and Darley's study by replacing the IV of 'other people' with an IV of 'gender'. Condition A consisted of 25 males, condition B 25 females. All the participants completed their questionnaires individually, alone in a room. They introduced another modification too, for practical reasons. Instead of using Latane and Darley's 'smoking grille effect', Terry and Geri created their emergency by sounding their college fire alarm. Their research rationale was: **A study to find out if there's a difference between the average response times of males and females in an emergency situation.** This converted into an experimental hypothesis that predicted: **There will be a difference between the average***

Box 4A Response times for Terry and Geri's participants, measured in seconds

---

Condition A (male)
4, 5, 5, 6, 8, 8, 8, 8, 9, 9, 10, 10, 10, 10, 11, 11, 11, 11, 11, 11, 12, 12, 13, 14, 14

Condition B (female)
1, 1, 3, 3, 4, 4, 5, 5, 6, 6, 6, 6, 7, 7, 7, 7, 8, 8, 8, 8, 10, 11, 12, 18, 21

response times of male and female participants in an emergency situation.

Box 4A shows Terry and Geri's **raw scores**. This term is used by psychologists to refer to **research results that are yet to have descriptive or inferential statistics applied to them**. When you see raw scores from a psychology study you usually see every single participant's score, presented in the form of lists. You'll notice that the scores in **Box 4A** have been set out in order, from lowest to highest. Otherwise, these raw scores are 'unsummarised' or, if you prefer, 'uncooked'. They're yet to be subjected to the rigours of our **two kinds of statistics**.

*Isn't it time you explained what these **two kinds of statistics** are?*

Yes. Here goes. **Descriptive statistics** are used by researchers to make raw scores easier to digest. They're used to **encapsulate the most important findings from a study** in manageable, bite-size chunks, as an alternative to presenting readers with long lists of raw data. Descriptive statistics are good news for anyone who reads *research reports*, since they reduce large amounts of data to much smaller helpings. They also make data more presentable, easier on the eye – in short, they summarise. A common use of descriptive statistics is to show the *average score* of a group of participants, rather than showing every individual score. So in their *research report* Terry and Geri might include the *average response times* for males and females, rather than simply listing all 50 raw scores and letting you work it out for yourself.

Inferential statistics are used for reasons associated less with *presentation* and more with *confidence*. When researchers come up with an experimental hypothesis they make a prediction about how a *sample* of participants will behave in a certain situation. If the research findings support the prediction, they'll conclude – with a high degree of *confidence* – that everyone in their *population* would behave in a similar way in a similar situation (use Chapter 3 to check the precise meanings of *samples* and *populations*). In other words, they'll *generalise* their findings from their sample to their population.

Researchers make predictions about the effect of independent variables (*IVs*) upon dependent variables (*DVs*). Typically they predict that a change in the value of their *DV* will be attributable to a change in the value of their *IV*, whilst extraneous variables (*EVs*) are held constant (the section on *laboratory experiments* in Chapter 3 has a detailed explanation of these variables).

Terry and Geri are researching the effect of gender (IV) and response time (DV). If their findings support their hypothesis they'll conclude that any differences in the response times of their two conditions are attributable to gender. Furthermore, they'll conclude that these differences exist in the population as well as in their sample.

But wait. Isn't there a problem with making conclusions like these?

Yes, there is. What if the difference in the response times of Terry and Geri's conditions *isn't* due to gender at all? What if it's due to something else? Chance, for instance. What if, *just by chance*, their female condition reacts more quickly than their male condition? After all, even if they'd used two male groups (instead of a male group and a female group) there would almost certainly be *some* difference between the reaction times of the two groups – owing to chance, random variation.

So Terry and Geri have a problem here. How can they defend themselves against the claim that the difference in the value of their *DV* between the two conditions isn't attributable to their *IV*, but to chance, random variation? The answer is, by using **inferential statistics**.

Researchers use **inferential statistics** to **demonstrate that a change in the value of a dependent variable can be confidently attributed to a change in the value of an independent variable, rather than to chance, random variation**. Inferential statistics enable researchers to be more *confident* about generalising their findings from a *sample* to a *population*.

Sounds like a useful safety net. So how do inferential statistics work?

Skills for using **inferential statistics** in psychological research are dealt with in the second section of this chapter. First, though, a guide to the *other* kind of statistics.

▶ Descriptive statistics

Descriptive statistics reduce large amounts of data to smaller, more manageable helpings. One common way of doing this is to work out the *average, middle or most typical score* for a group of participants in a study. This enables you to condense a long list of raw scores to a single value. These **average, middle or most typical scores for a set** are called **measures of central tendency**.

Three measures of central tendency

The mean is the **average score for a set**. To calculate the mean for a set of scores, add up all the scores in the set, then divide your total by the number of scores in the set. **Box 4B** shows how to work out the mean for Terry and Geri's male condition.

The median is the **middle score in a set**. To work out the median, set out all the scores in sequence, from lowest to highest. The median value is the number that lies half way along the sequence. So if there are five scores in a set, the median is the *third* number in the sequence. **Box 4C** shows you how to calculate the median for Terry and Geri's males.

Wait a minute. What happens if you have a set that has an even number of scores in it? How do you find the middle value in a set of, say, six scores?

Good question. In cases like these the median value is halfway between the *middle two numbers*. So in a set of six scores like 3, 4, 6, 7, 8, 9 the median is halfway between 6 and 7. So it's 6.5.

The Mode is the **most typical score for a set**. To spot the mode in a set, simply see which value occurs most frequently. **Box 4D** shows the mode for Terry and Geri's males.

Box 4B   Working out the mean for *condition* A in Terry and Geri's study

---

Step 1   Add up all the scores in the set:

$4 + 5 + 5 + 6 + 8 + 8 + 8 + 8 + 9 + 9 + 10 + 10 + 10 + 10 + 11 + 11$
$+ 11 + 11 + 11 + 11 + 11 + 12 + 12 + 13 + 14 + 14 = 241$

Step 2   Divide the total by the number of scores in the set:

$241 \div 25 = 9.64$

The **mean** response time for males in Terry and Geri's study is 9.64 seconds.

Box 4C   Working out the median for *condition A* in Terry and Geri's study

> **Step 1**   Set out all the scores in the set in order, from lowest to highest:
>
> 4, 5, 5, 6, 8, 8, 8, 8, 9, 9, 10, 10, 10, 10, 11, 11, 11, 11, 11, 11, 12, 12, 13, 14, 14
>
> **Step 2**   Find the number that lies at the midpoint in the set:
>
> 4, 5, 5, 6, 8, 8, 8 ,8, 9, 9, 10, 10, **10**, 10, 11,11, 11, 11, 11, 11, 12, 12, 13, 14, 14
>
> The **median** response time for males in this study is 10 seconds.

Box 4D   Working out the mode for *condition A* in Terry and Geri's study

> Simply find the most commonly occurring score in the set:
>
> 4, 5, 5, 6, 8, 8, 8, 8, 9, 9, 10, 10, 10, 10, **11, 11, 11, 11, 11, 11**, 12, 12, 13, 14, 14
>
> The **mode** response time for males in Terry and Geri's experiment is 11 seconds.

Wait. What if you have a set of scores that has two most frequently occurring values, for example, as in this set: 3, 6, 6, 6, 7, 8, 8, 8? How do you select the mode then?

In unusual cases like these you call the set a **bi-modal set – a set of scores that has two modal scores**. Another unusual case is where you have a set of scores with **no mode**. For example, in a set like *4, 5, 6, 7, 8, 9*. Here you'd have to say there's *no modal score*.

Mean, median and mode complement each other quite nicely
If you've had your eyes peeled you'll have noticed that these three measures of central tendency give three different values for the scores in Terry and Geri's male condition. Since the mean, median and mode

are all worked out differently, this shouldn't be too much of a surprise. In fact, although mean, median and mode are all measures of central tendency, they don't all do the same thing. They each reveal *something different* about the set. The mean reveals the *average* score. The median reveals the *middle* score. The mode reveals the *most typical* score. And since each one tells us something that the other two don't, you could say **the mean, median and mode complement each other quite nicely**.

The mean is a very popular measure of central tendency, but median and mode are pretty useful too
Occasionally the mean, median and mode *are* all the same. This happens when a set of scores approximates **a normal distribution**. This 'special case' comes up for discussion later in this section, so I won't dwell on it here. For now it's sufficient to say that when your research throws up a set of scores, you have a choice of three measures for working out its central tendency. You might choose to use one of them, two of them, or all three. The choice you make will depend on *what you want to know about your scores*. Researchers usually find the *average* score to be the most useful measure of central tendency, so they plump for the mean. No doubt the **mean is a very popular measure of central tendency**, **but median and mode are pretty useful too**. Indeed, on many occasions a mixture of more than one measure of central tendency is effective. Here are some examples:

- **Example 1   When the median is a useful complement to the mean**
  What if Terry and Geri's male condition had an extra participant who dozed off and consequently took 5 minutes to react to the emergency? His extreme, 'outlying' score dramatically alters the mean value for the set. Now the mean is 20.8 seconds, instead of 9.64 seconds. Whilst this mean value still gives the true average score for the set, as a measure of central tendency it's rather misleading. In this kind of situation, where a set has an extreme, untypical 'outlying' score, the median is a useful complement to the mean. The median score for the set, including the dozing participant, is 10. It's unaffected by the extreme 'outlier'.

- **Example 2   When the mode is a useful complement to the mean**

Look again at Terry and Geri's male condition. It has a mean of 9.64. Let's round it up to 10 for the moment. In this set, four males scored 10. But what if two of these had scored 9, not 10? And what if another two had scored 11, not 10? Now we have a situation where the mean remains 10, yet nobody actually scored 10. So although the mean gives true average value, it doesn't tell us what most people scored. Indeed, it doesn't tell us what anyone scored. It may well be that Terry and Geri are interested in what the most popular, most typical score was. If so, the mode would be a useful complement to the mean.

- **Example 3   The mean is not even an option**
  If a set of scores is presented at the **ordinal** or **nominal levels of measurement**, it's impossible to calculate their mean, so the median or mode are used as measures of central tendency. Only scores at the **interval level** can be used to calculate a mean value (**interval**, **ordinal** and **nominal levels of measurement** are dealt with in some detail in the second half of this chapter).

Measures of central tendency are usually presented alongside **measures of how well spread a set of scores is**. These measures of spread are called **measures of dispersion**. They show whoever's reading your *research report* whether the scores in a set are all clustered around a central point, or whether they're spread out. The combination of central tendency and dispersion gives a well-rounded picture of how the scores in a set are distributed. Presenting one without the other is frowned upon by most psychology tutors.

Three measures of dispersion
The range is the most straightforward way to work out the spread of a set of scores. It's **the difference between the highest and lowest scores**. Work out the range by subtracting the lowest score from the highest. **Box 4E** shows you how to calculate the range for Terry and Geri's male condition.

   The mean deviation gives **the mean of the deviations from the mean**. In other words, it states the average amount by which all scores in a set differ (deviate) from the average. To work out mean deviation, first find the mean for a set of scores. Then work out by how much each individual score deviates from the mean. Finally, calculate the mean of all these deviations. **Box 4F** shows the mean deviation calculation for Terry and Geri's males.

Box 4E   Working out the range for *condition A* in Terry and Geri's study

---

Step 1   Set out all the scores in the set in sequence, from lowest to highest:

4, 5, 5, 6, 8, 8, 8, 8, 9, 9, 10, 10, 10, 10, 11, 11, 11, 11, 11, 11, 12, 12, 13, 14, **14**.

Step 2   Subtract the lowest score from the highest score:

14 − 4 = 10.

The **range** of response times for males in Terry and Geri's study is 10 seconds.

Mean deviation is seldom used

Although it's easy to calculate, as a measure of dispersion **mean deviation is seldom used**. Mathematicians regard *ignoring all the negative and positive signs when totalling the deviations for individual scores* as a rather clumsy manoeuvre that's best avoided. Consequently, **standard deviation** is a more respectable measure of dispersion.

The standard deviation **(SD)** is **a way of working out dispersion in a more mathematically sophisticated way than by using mean deviation**. Using *SD* enables you to avoid the rather clumsy manoeuvre of *ignoring all the positive and negative signs* when totalling the deviations for the individual scores. *SD* can be calculated in seven steps, as follows:

Step 1: Find the mean for the set of scores. **Step 2**: Work out how much each score deviates from the mean by subtracting the mean from each score. **Step 3**: Square each of the deviation values from *step 2*. **Step 4**: Add up all the squared values from *step 3* to give you *the sum of the squares*. **Step 5**: Subtract 1 from the number of scores in the set to give you *N − 1*. **Step 6**: Divide *the sum of the squares* by *N − 1*. This gives you the **variance** of the set of scores. **Step 7**: Find the square root of the **variance** to give you the *SD* for the set.

Standard deviation throws up a couple of questions

Before applying this procedure to Terry and Geri's scores (see **Box 4G**) you may feel that *SD* **throws up a couple of questions** that need

Box 4F Working out the mean deviation for *condition A* in Terry and Geri's study

---

Step 1 Find the mean for the set: 9.64.

Step 2 Work out how much each individual score deviates from the mean. Do this by subtracting the mean from each score. In the list below, the figures in brackets are the deviations for each score.

4(–5.64), 5(–4.64), 5(–4.64), 6(–3.64), 8(–1.64), 8(–1.64), 8(–1.64), 8(–1.64), 9(–0.64), 9(0.64), 10(+0.36), 10(+0.36), 10(+0.36), 10(+0.36), 11(+1.36), 11(+1.36), 11(+1.36), 11(+1.36), 11(+1.36), 11(+1.36), 12(+2.36), 12(+2.36), 13(+3.36), 14(+4.36), 14(+4.36).

Step 3 Work out the mean of all the deviations. Do this by adding all the deviations together, *ignoring all the positive and negative signs*, then dividing the total by the *number* of deviations:

5.64 + 4.64 + 4.64 + 3.64 + 1.64 + 1.64 + 1.64 + 1.64 + 0.64 + 0.64 + 0.36 + 0.36 + 0.36 + 0.36 + 1.36 + 1.36 + 1.36 + 1.36 + 1.36 + 1.36 + 2.36 + 2.36 + 3.36 + 4.36 + 4.36 = 52.8   52.8 ÷ 25 = 2.1.

The **mean deviation** for Terry and Geri's male participants is 2.1 seconds.

---

answering. Firstly, what's **variance**? Well, it's the term used to refer to **the square of standard deviation**. Variance is sometimes used as a measure of dispersion in its own right, though here we're using it as a step on the way to calculating *SD*. Second question: when calculating *SD* why do we divide *the sum of the squares* by $N - 1$ and not by N (the number of deviations)? Well, dividing by $N - 1$ rather than N *raises the value* of the variance and *SD* for a set. It produces a measure of dispersion that's a little on the *generous* side. The reason for this generosity is that we're calculating the standard deviation for a *sample* of scores, rather than for an entire *population* (see Chapter 3 for an explanation of samples and populations). And since **the scores for a sample are unlikely to be perfectly representative of the scores for a population**, we tend to slightly inflate our estimate of variance and *SD* to allow for this discrepancy (or **sampling error**, as it's often called). This means we can be more confident about generalising our measure of dispersion to the entire population.

Box 4G Working out the SD for *condition A* in Terry and Geri's study

---

Step 1 Find the mean for the set of scores: 9.64.

Step 2 Work out how much each score deviates from the mean by subtracting the mean from each score. The figures in brackets are the deviations for each score:

4(–5.64), 5(–4.64), 5(–4.64), 6(–3.64), 8(–1.64), 8(–1.64), 8(–1.64), 8(–1.64), 9(–0.64), 9(–0.64), 10(+0.36), 10(+0.36), 10(+0.36), 10(+0.36), 11(+1.36), 11(+1.36), 11(+1.36), 11(+1.36), 11(+1.36), 11(+1.36), 12(+2.36), 12(+2.36), 13(+3.36), 14(+4.36), 14(+4.36).

Step 3 Square each of the deviation values from *step 2*. In the list below, the figures in brackets are the squared deviations for each score:

4(31.8), 5(21.5), 5(21.5), 6(13.2), 8(2.7), 8(2.7), 8(2.7), 8(2.7), 9(0.4), 9(0.4), 10(0.1), 10(0.1), 10(0.1), 10(0.1), 11(1.8), 11(1.8), 11(1.8), 11(1.8), 11(1.8), 11(1.8), 12(5.6), 12(5.6), 13(11.3), 14(19.0), 14(19.0).

Step 4 Add up all the squared values from *step 3* to give the sum of the squares:

31.8 + 21.5 + 21.5 + 13.2 + 2.7 + 2.7 + 2.7 + 2.7 + 0.4 + 0.4 + 0.1 + 0.1 + 0.1 + 0.1 + 1.8 + 1.8 + 1.8 + 1.8 + 1.8 + 1.8 + 5.6 + 5.6 + 11.3 + 19.0 + 19.0 = 171.3.

Step 5 Subtract 1 from the number of scores in the set to give N – 1: 25 – 1 = 24.

Step 6 Divide the sum of the squares by N – 1 to give the variance of the set:

171.3 ÷ 24 = 7.1.

Step 7 Find the square root of the variance to give the SD for the set:

$\sqrt{7.1} = 2.7$

The **standard deviation** for Terry and Geri's male participants is 2.7.

Not all measures of dispersion are equally useful
It was suggested a few paragraphs ago that mean deviation is seldom used. You'd be right to conclude from this that **not all measures of dispersion are equally useful**. However, the *range* and *SD* both have their uses, depending on *what you want to know about your scores*. If you want a quick, easy way to work out how widely spread a set is, the range is ideal. If you want a measure of dispersion that's sensitive to every value in your set, *SD* is the popular choice. But since these two measures *tell you different things* about how a set is dispersed, you may want to use them both. Like mean, median and mode, they complement each other quite nicely.

Now you're skilled in working out measures of central tendency and dispersion, you may want to 'please the eye' of whoever's reading your *research report* with some **graphical summaries** of your participants' scores. **Graphs for summarising sets of scores** can be used *alongside* measures of central tendency and dispersion. This combination of 'pictures and numbers' neatly encapsulates your data in a way that's both informative and attractive to look at. There are several ways of summarising scores using graphs. Three popular ones are suggested below.

Three ways of summarising scores graphically
The first two are **histograms** and **bar charts**. I'll introduce these together, since they have plenty in common.
   Histograms are graphs that show how frequently scores appear in a set. Each *individual score* can be represented by an interval along the horizontal axis. The *frequency* of each score's appearance in the set is shown by a tower extending up the vertical axis. Where you have a large number of individual scores you can create **grouped scores along the horizontal axis**. These grouped scores are called **class intervals**. This way, each group of scores (class interval) is represented by a separate tower. **Box 4H** has two examples of histograms, one for each of Terry and Geri's conditions: **4H(a)** uses *individual scores* on the horizontal axis, **4H(b)** uses *class intervals*.
   Bar charts have a lot in common with histograms. Like histograms, they **show the frequency of a particular variable**. In other words, they can tell the reader how often a particular event occurs in a study. Also like histograms they use vertical towers (bars) to indicate *frequency*. For example, the bar chart in **Box 4I** shows how frequently males and females in Terry and Geri's study responded to the emergency in under ten seconds. As well as showing the *frequency* of a vari-

Box 4H   Histograms showing scores for Terry and Geri's *conditions A* and *B*

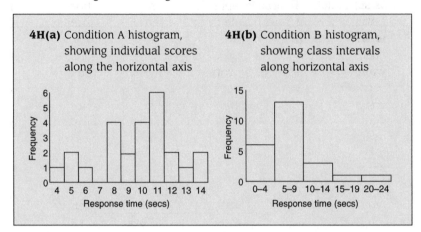

4H(a) Condition A histogram, showing individual scores along the horizontal axis

4H(b) Condition B histogram, showing class intervals along horizontal axis

able, bar charts can be used to compare mean scores, percentage scores, proportions and so forth.

There is a key difference between histograms and bar charts and this will affect which one you decide to use
What you've read so far should tell you that these two types of graphs have plenty in common. However, **there is a key difference between histograms and bar charts and this will affect which one you decide to use.** It concerns the kinds of variables that appear along their horizontal axes. **Along the horizontal axes of histograms you'll find numerically ordered variables**. Typical examples of these are time and temperature. Variables like these are measured at what's called the **interval level of measurement** (the second half of this chapter has an explanation of **levels of measurement**). Since histograms have *continuous variables* along their horizontal axes, their towers are shown side by side, with no gaps between them. **Along the horizontal axes of bar charts you'll find discrete, discontinuous variables,** for example, gender. Gender has just two values (male or female) rather than a *sequence* of values along a continuum. Variables like these are measured at the **nominal level of measurement** (see the second half of this chapter). Other examples of *discrete, discontinuous variables* are eye colour and nationality. As bar charts show *discontinuous variables* along their horizontal axes, their towers are separated. They have gaps between them. Look out for the horizontal axis on the bar chart in **Box 4I**.
   Pie charts are a third way of summarising scores graphically.

Box 4I Bar chart showing how frequently Terry and Geri's males and females responded in under 10 seconds

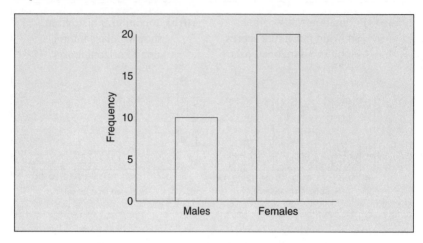

They're useful when you want to **show how a particular variable divides up proportionally between a number of groups**. In effect, they show 'how big a piece of pie' each particular group has. The pie charts in **Box 4J** show the results of an exit questionnaire Terry and Geri gave to their participants. They were asked to indicate whether they had felt *very scared, a little scared* or *not at all scared* during the emergency situation.

Measures of central tendency and dispersion, as well as the graphical summaries covered here, are all useful ways of *describing* research data. Thanks to these *descriptive statistics*, your *research report* will be more concise and easier on the eye. Before crossing the border from *descriptive statistics* to *inferential statistics* there's one more idea to explore. It's another handy tool for *describing* data, but it also provides a key to unlock some of the puzzles that lie in wait in the second half of this chapter.

The normal distribution
*Let's say Terry and Geri repeat their experiment on a larger scale. Rather than having 50 participants, let's say their follow-up study has 100 participants: 50 males, 50 females. And let's say the histogram in **Box 4K** shows the reaction times for the male and female participants in this second, larger experiment.*

Box 4J Pie charts showing reported fear levels of Terry and Geri's participants

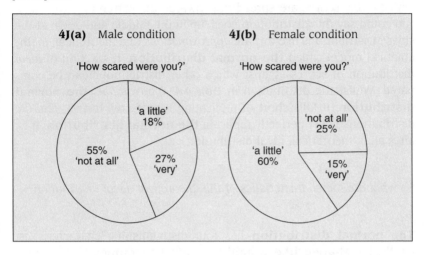

4J(a) Male condition

'How scared were you?'

'a little'
18%

55%
'not at all'

27%
'very'

4J(b) Female condition

'How scared were you?'

'not at all'
25%

'a little'
60%

15%
'very'

Box 4K Histogram showing reaction times for participants in Terry and Geri's follow-up study

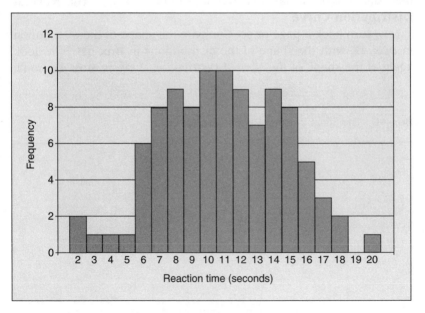

Terry and Geri's follow-up study shows a distribution in which *a lot* of scores are clustered around a central score of 10 to 12 seconds, whilst *a few* scores are spread out towards the extremities (or tails). You could say this distribution goes 'up in the middle and down at the sides'. Distributions like this are *approximations* of a theoretical, mathematical model called **the normal distribution**. It's a kind of *ideal* distribution of scores against which other distributions can be compared. Whilst the distribution in **Box 4K** *approximates* **the normal distribution**, it falls short of replicating it perfectly. In fact, *real life* distributions never perfectly replicate **the normal distribution**. It is, after all, a theoretical, ideal distribution.

So what are the characteristics of this theoretical, ideal distribution?

The normal distribution has four distinguishing characteristics. *Firstly*, it's **shaped like a bell**. *Secondly* it's **symmetrical**. *Thirdly*, the **mean, median and mode for the set are the same**. *Fourthly*, its **extremities (tails) don't touch the horizontal axis**, but carry on out towards infinity. **Box 4L** shows the shape of this theoretical, ideal distribution. It has a shape that's often known as **the Normal Distribution Curve**.

Now turn back a page or so. Compare the shape of the distribution in **Box 4K** with the shape of the distributions in **Box 4H**. Now look again at the shape of *the Normal Distribution Curve* in **Box 4L**. You'll

Box 4L   The 'ideal' Normal Distribution Curve

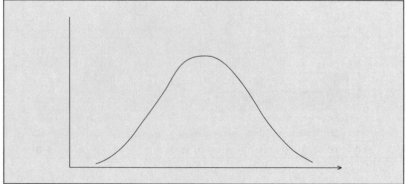

notice that whilst none of the distributions in **4H** or **4K** perfectly replicate *the Normal Distribution Curve*, the one in **4K** provides the *closest approximation* to it. Actually, neither of the distributions in **4H** are symmetrical, since they both 'lean' to the left. **Asymmetrical, leaning distributions** like these are sometimes called **skewed distributions**.

A key reason why **Box 4K** resembles *the Normal Distribution Curve* more closely than **Box 4H** does, is that **4K** describes a set that has more scores in it than **4H** does. After all, the histogram in **4K** includes scores from 100 participants, whereas those in **4H** show scores from only 25. In fact, for many of the variables psychologists are interested in (like reaction time, problem-solving ability, memory performance), as well as lots of other variables relating to human characteristics (such as height, weight, shoe size), it's generally true to say that *the more scores there are in a set, the greater the probability that its shape will closely resemble* the Normal Distribution Curve.

If you have a set of scores that *closely approximates* a normal distribution you can make a number of assumptions about your data:

- **Assumption 1**   *50 per cent of the scores in the set fall above the mean, 50 per cent below it*

  This one's fairly obvious when you consider that *the Normal Distribution Curve* is symmetrical. However, coming up are some other, less obvious assumptions that can be made about sets that *closely approximate* normal distribution. First, though, a short but necessary digression about the link between two closely related concepts.

  The link between standard deviation and something called z-scores: as you know, standard deviation (*SD*) is a measure of dispersion. For the scores in Terry and Geri's follow-up study, the mean reaction time is 10.9 seconds, the *SD* (calculated using the formula featured earlier in this chapter) is 2.4 seconds. From this we can say that a score of 13.3 (10.9 plus 2.4) lies *1 SD above the mean*, a score of 8.5 (10.9 minus 2.4) lies *1 SD below the mean*, 15.7 lies *2 SDs above the mean*, 6.1 lies *2 SDs below the mean* and so on.

  Now we're only a hair's breadth from discovering **the link between standard deviation and something called *z-scores*.** A **z-score** is **a measure of how many *SD*s a score lies above or below the mean**. In our example, a score of 13.3 *has a z-score of +1*, 8.5 *has a z-score of −1*, 15.7 *has a z-score of +2* and so on.

Now, back to those assumptions about sets of scores that *closely approximate* a normal distribution:

- **Assumption 2**   *68.26 per cent of scores always fall within 1 SD above and below the mean.*

- **Assumption 3**   *31.74 per cent of scores always fall beyond 1 SD above and below the mean.*

These assumptions are often referred to as **the properties of the area under the Normal Distribution Curve**. They apply to all sets of scores that *closely approximate* a normal distribution. Treat them as statistical 'facts of life'. **Box 4M** summarises them.

About these z-scores. Are they useful?

For working out the position of a particular score in relation to the other scores in a set that closely approximates a normal distribution, they're really useful. They enable you to calculate *what proportion of scores (in an approximately normally distributed set) lie between a given score and the mean.* They also enable you to calculate *what proportion of scores (in an approximately normally distributed set) are higher or lower than a given score.*

Box 4M   The properties of the area under the Normal Distribution Curve

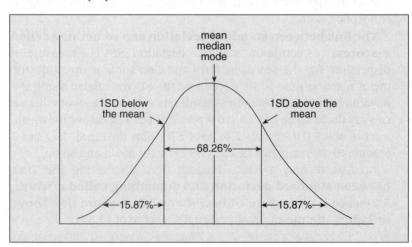

For example, imagine you're a participant in Terry and Geri's follow-up study. And imagine your reaction time is 9 seconds. So your score deviates from the mean (11) by 2 seconds. Another way of putting this is to say that you have a *deviation score* of –2 (which has a negative sign because it lies *below* the mean). Now, to work out your z-score, simply *divide your deviation score by the SD for the set*: –2 divided by 3.6 = –0.6. You have a z-score of –0.6. This means your score lies 0.6 *SDs below the mean*. Now, assuming the set *closely approximates* a normal distribution, you can find out *what proportion of scores lies between your score and the mean*, or *what proportion of scores is higher or lower than yours*, by using the table in Appendix 3.

How to decide whether a set of scores closely approximates a normal distribution

You already know that a normal distribution is an ideal that never properly models real-life scores. And you already know that some real-life sets *approximate* normal distribution more closely than others do. However, you may not yet know **how to decide whether or not a set of scores closely approximates a normal distribution**. This is a skill worth having, whether you're working with *descriptive* statistics or in the neighbouring territory of *inferential* statistics. After all, the z-score manipulations featured above can only be performed on so called *normally distributed* sets, in other words, sets that are close approximations to a normal distribution. And as you'll discover in the second section of this chapter, there are some inferential manipulations that only apply to sets that *closely approximate a normal distribution*. So how *do* you decide whether a set *closely approximates* a normal distribution? Here are two methods.

First, use an **eye-ball test**. To 'eye-ball' a set of scores, first draw a histogram, then **look at the shape of the distribution** to see if it *closely approximates the Normal Distribution Curve*. Does it go up in the middle and down at the sides? Is it *approximately* symmetrical? Is it *approximately* shaped like a bell? Are the mean, median and mode *approximately* the same? If the answers to these questions are 'yes' 'yes', 'yes' and 'yes' respectively, you can safely say your set *closely approximates* a normal distribution. For most psychology tutors, 'eye-balling' is an accurate enough test of close approximation.

Alternatively, use a **goodness of fit test**. This is **a statistical test for establishing how closely a given set of scores conforms to the ideal, normally distributed set.** You'll find an example of a goodness of fit test in Appendix 4. These are best used where an eye-ball test leaves you undecided about close approximation. They're very much for the perfectionist.

Before crossing the border into the other half of this chapter, the half where statistics are used for making *inferences* about data rather than for *describing* it, make sure you've grasped each of the key terms in **Box 4N.**

Box 4N   Using descriptive statistics: A–Z of terms to remember

Bar charts are graphs that show the frequency of a particular variable. Along the horizontal axes of bar charts you'll find discrete, discontinuous variables.

Bi-modal sets are scores that have two modal values.

Correlation co-efficients are numbers for measuring the strength of the correlation between two variables (introduced in Chapter 3).

Descriptive statistics encapsulate the most important findings from a study.

Dispersion measures how well spread a set of scores is.

Histograms are graphs that show how frequently scores appear in a set. Along the horizontal axes of histograms you'll find continuous, numerical variables.

Mean is the average score in a set.

Mean deviation is the mean of the deviations from the mean in a set.

Measures of central tendency are average, middle, or most typical scores for a set.

Median is the middle score in a set.

Mode is the most typical score in a set.

Normal distribution is a theoretical, mathematical model in which a lot of scores are clustered around a central point and a few scores are spread out towards the extremities.

Pie charts show how a variable divides up proportionally between a number of groups.

Range is the difference between the highest and lowest scores in a set.

Box 4N *Continued*

Raw data are research results that haven't had descriptive or inferential statistics applied to them.

Sampling errors happen when sample scores are unrepresentative of a population's scores.

Skewed distributions are asymmetrical distributions.

Standard deviation is a way of working out dispersion in a more mathematically sophisticated way than by using mean deviation.

Variance is the square of standard deviation.

Z-scores measure how many *SD*s a score lies above or below the mean for a set.

▶ Inferential statistics

Now turn back a few pages. The opening section of this chapter outlines the aims of inferential statistics. After reading this outline you'd be right to regard statistics of inference as a kind of 'researchers' defence' against anyone who might attribute the findings from a study to chance, random variation, rather than to the influence of an independent variable (*IV*) on a dependent variable (*DV*).

Sounds like a useful safety net. So how do inferential statistics work?

To answer this question let's stick with the case of Terry and Geri's original study on *male and female responses to an emergency situation* (the first half of this chapter has a full account of this study).

Terry and Geri's hypothesis predicts that **there will be a difference between the average response times of male and female participants in an emergency situation.** *Their results show that there is a difference. The mean response time for* condition A *is 9.64 seconds. For* B *it's 7.28 seconds. Females, on average, responded more quickly than males.*

Having observed a difference between the response times of their *samples*, Terry and Geri would like to *generalise* these findings to the *populations* from which their samples are drawn. But they'll only be justified in doing so *if the difference between their two sample means is big enough* – or, as researchers prefer to put it, *significant* enough – for them to do so.

Who decides if the difference between their two sample means is significant enough?

Researchers decide for themselves, by applying **inferential tests** to their data. More will be revealed about **inferential tests** shortly. First, though, a short but necessary digression on the subject of *hypotheses*. Did you know there are different types?

Hypotheses

A testable prediction about the outcome of a study is called a *research hypothesis* or *experimental hypothesis*. But this isn't the only type of prediction in the researcher's repertoire. In fact, *there are different varieties of hypotheses* you're likely to hear about whilst mixing with psychological researchers. One is the **null hypothesis**. Null hypotheses predict the *opposite* of research hypotheses. If a research hypothesis predicts a *difference* between two samples of scores on a particular variable, the **null hypothesis** predicts that there will be *no difference*. In fact, the **null hypothesis** is sometimes called the **prediction of no difference**. When you have research findings that *support* a research hypothesis it's customary – according to statistical convention – to say that you *reject the null hypothesis.* This simply means that the prediction of no difference has been thrown out.

Two other types of prediction are **one-tailed** and **two-tailed hypotheses**. The first of these is very specific, the second isn't. **One-tailed hypotheses specify the *direction* in which an *IV* will influence a *DV*.** For instance, they specify that a change in an *IV* will *either* increase *or* decrease the value of a *DV*. **Two-tailed hypotheses predict that an *IV* will influence a *DV,* but they don't specify the direction**. In other words, they predict that a change in the *IV* will influence the *DV*, but the direction of change isn't specified.

Researchers who use one-tailed hypotheses are generally pretty confident about the direction of influence of their *IV* over their *DV*. A word of warning, though. Your choice of a one- or two-tailed hypothesis influences the kind of **inferential test** you'll apply to your data, so be sure you know *which is which and which one you're using for your research*.

In Terry and Geri's study the null hypothesis predicts that **there will be no difference between the response times of the two conditions**. *A closer look at the research hypothesis for this study reveals it to be* **two-tailed**. *It predicts that response time (DV) will be influenced by gender (IV) but it doesn't specify whether male or female response times will be higher. A one-tailed hypothesis for this study would be* **females will respond more quickly to the emergency situation than males will**.

So what are these **inferential tests**?

I'll come to them presently. First, a word about **errors**.

Error
As in most fields, human error flourishes in the field of inferential statistics. So you need to have your wits about you. But *researchers who use inferential statistics are prone to two types of errors* in particular. First, there's the **type one error**. This error results from being overly optimistic. Researchers who claim their results are *significant* – that they are attributable to the effect of an *IV* on a *DV* when in fact they're simply the result of chance, random variation – are committing a **type one error**. In short, they're **rejecting a null hypothesis that should be accepted**. Then there's the **type two error**: this is the opposite of the type one error. Researchers who claim their results have come about because of chance, random variation when they're attributable to the influence of their *IV* on their *DV* are making a **type two error**. They're **accepting a null hypothesis that should be rejected**. You could say this error comes from being overly pessimistic.

If Terry and Geri attribute the difference in response times between their male and female conditions to gender (IV) when in fact it came about by chance, random variation, they'd be making a **type one error**.

What about these **inferential tests**?

All in good time. First, a word about something called **the 5 per cent level of significance**.

The 5 per cent level of significance
Imagine you've done a piece of research and obtained sets of scores for two conditions. Your *two-tailed* research hypothesis predicts a dif-

ference between the two sets. Your *null hypothesis* predicts no differ-ence. Let's say there *is* a difference, but you're not sure it's big enough to make your results *significant*. To find out whether it *is* big enough you do an **inferential test** on your data. Based on the outcome of this test, you go ahead and *reject your null hypothesis*. Now pause for a moment and ask yourself a question: *what's the probability that you've rejected a null hypothesis you should have accepted?* In other words, *what's the probability that you've made a type one error?* Gen-erally researchers *set* this level of probability at 5 per cent. This means there's 1 in 20 chance of wrongly rejecting the null hypothesis. This is **the 5 per cent level of significance**. It's **a *set* 'level of doubt' that researchers conventionally operate at when rejecting null hypotheses**. When you do an **inferential test** on your data you'll arrive at a statistical value which may show your results to be *signifi-cant* at the 5% level. If they *are* significant at this level, you'll reject your null hypothesis. But you'll do so with a 5 per cent 'level of doubt', a 1 in 20 chance that you've made a type one error. An interesting consequence of this '5 per cent convention' is that **psychologists who reject null hypotheses are only 95 per cent sure of what they're saying**.

Terry and Geri have observed a difference between the mean scores of their two conditions. To find out whether the difference is significant they'll select an **inferential test***. This will throw up a statistical value which they'll check against the 5 per cent level of significance. If they find there to be a less then 1 in 20 chance that they'll make a type one error, they'll reject their null hypothesis and conclude that in the popu-lation at large, female responses to emergencies are significantly faster than male responses.*

Isn't it high time you explained these **inferential tests***?*

Almost. First, though, some thoughts about something called **levels of measurement**. A sprinter's success can be quantified in different ways. What's her fastest time? What's her world ranking? Is she in the Olympic team? Similarly, participants' behaviour in psychological research can be quantified in different ways – three main ways in fact, called **levels of measurement**. The reason for these different *levels* is that *different research situations call for behaviour to be quan-tified in different ways*. And the *level* at which behaviour is quanti-fied in a study will determine how its data are presented, that is, what form they're presented in. In short, **levels of measurement** are **different ways of quantifying behaviour and presenting research data**. The level of measurement used by a researcher has a bearing on the kind of **inferential test** that will be applied to it, so be sure you know *which is which and which one you're using for your research*.

Three levels of measurement

First, there's **the nominal level**. Here, **data is presented in separate, discrete groups**. If you participate in a study that measures behaviour at this level your performance leads to your being put into one of a number of *separate, discrete* groups (*separate* and *discrete* in that each participant is placed in *one group or another*, not at some point in between). For example, after a spelling test you might be put into a 'pass' group or a 'fail' group. For another example, a set of children could be divided according to their eye colour – blue, brown, green, and so on. In studies like these the researcher wants to know the number (*frequency*) of participants in each *separate, discrete* group. In the 'spelling' example, participants are divided into *two* groups. This is very common, though some (more complex) studies use more than two.

The second level is **the ordinal level**. Here, **data is presented in rank order**. As a participant in a study using the ordinal level you're given a *rank position* (like 2nd or 5th or 50th) to show how you faired on whatever variable was measured. An ordinal score shows *your position relative to the other participants in the group*, as opposed to *which group you belong to*, which is what a nominal score shows.

The third level is **the interval level**. Here, **data is presented as scores on a scale with equal units**. As a participant in a study with interval data you find out *how much better or worse than the other participants* you did, rather than just being given a *rank position*. So instead of finding out that she was the 5th fastest in her race, the sprinter finds out her *actual score* or *time*. From this she can work out *how much* faster she was than the 6th fastest runner. Some examples of interval scales are *seconds* (for measuring time), metres (distance), kilos (weight) – All the widely used units of measurement. A key feature of interval level is that it uses scales that have *equal units*. This means that *each interval on the scale has the same value*. So on a scale that measures time in seconds the difference between 8 and 9 seconds *is equal to* the difference between 12 and 13 seconds or 17 and 18 seconds. This feature of the interval level of measurement has, from time to time, caused confusion.

Imagine you're a participant in a study involving a spelling test. You spell 16 out of a possible 20 words correctly. A fellow participant, Kim, spells 15 correctly. Two other participants, Tim and Sim, score 8 and 7 respectively. Now consider this question. *Is the difference in spelling performance between yourself and Kim equal to the difference in performance between Tim and Jim?* Probably not. Why not? Because the scale you're being measured on doesn't have *equal units* like a proper interval scale does. After all, it would be daft to say that the difference in 'spelling ability' between someone who scores 16 and someone who scores 8 *is equal to* the difference between someone who scores 8 and someone who scores zero. Only scales that have *equal* units are regarded as proper interval scales. So beware. **Some scales appear to present data at the interval level, even though they don't.** Famous and notorious examples are intelligence and personality scales, generically known as *psychometric* scales. They're perfectly legitimate in psychological research, though they're not regarded as proper interval scales. For the purposes of doing **inferential tests** it's conventional to 'downgrade' data from scales that appear – falsely – to present data at the interval level to the *next lowest* level of measurement. This means downgrading them to the *ordinal* level by giving each score a *rank position*. Appendix 5 has a guide to *ranking scores*.

Terry and Geri's measured response time (DV) in seconds. This is a widely used scale with equal units, so it's fine to regard it as an interval scale. Yet it might have been so different. Rather than recording each participants' time in seconds they might have given them all a rank position. The first to react would have been ranked 1, the last, rank 50. This would have been an ordinal scale. Then again, they might have divided their participants into two separate, discrete groups. One group that responded in' under 10 seconds', one that didn't. Then they'd have been using a nominal scale.

Inferential tests
Tests of inference **enable you to *infer***, from the data you've collected in your study, **whether or not your results are significant at the 5 per cent level**. In other words, they tell you whether or not to *reject your null hypothesis*.

Most of the inferential tests featured in this section are for working out if the *difference* between the scores in your conditions is big enough to be regarded as *statistically significant*. Tests that do this are sometimes called *tests of difference*. Two bonus tests are also featured in this section. These are specially designed tests for working out the significance of data from correlational studies. In other words, they're *tests for calculating correlation co-efficients* (Chapter 3 has a guide to the correlational – and other – methodologies).

The eight tests covered here should cater for all your inferential statistical needs, especially if you're still in the early stages of your research career.

Hang on. With eight tests to choose from, how do you decide which one to select?

Your choice of test will depend on *the nature of your study and on the kind of data it produced*. **Box 4P** offers you *a quick guide to selecting the appropriate inferential test for your data*. **Box 4Q** offers a *detailed guide* to the same. Be warned, selecting an *inappropriate* test may lead

Box 4P A quick guide to selecting the appropriate inferential test for your data

	Tests of difference		Tests for calculating correlation co-efficients
	Independent design	**Repeated measures _or_ Matched pairs**	
Nominal level	Chi-square (see Box 4S)	sign (see Box 4R)	
Ordinal level	Mann–Whitney U (see Box 4U)	Wilcoxon (see Box 4T)	Spearman's rho (see Box 4Z)
Interval level	Unrelated t (see Box 4W)	Related t (see Box 4V)	Pearson's product-moment calculation (see Box 4Y)

to your arriving at inappropriate conclusions about the *significance* of your data, which is frowned upon by tutors, lecturers and examiners alike. So make sure you know *which test is which and which one's best for your data*.

The *t-tests* on the bottom row of **Box 4P** are regarded as the most 'statistically powerful' of all the inferential tests included here. Sometimes these 'extra powerful' tests are called *parametric* tests. Predictably, the others are known as *non-parametric* tests. Once you've selected the appropriate test for your research, go ahead and apply it to your data. The rest of this chapter guides you through the calculations for the tests shown in **Boxes 4P** and **4Q**.

Box 4Q   A detailed guide to selecting the appropriate inferential test for your data

The most popular inferential 'tests of difference' are *the Sign test*, the *Chi-square test*, the Wilcoxon test, *the Mann–Whitney U-test*, *the unrelated t-test* and *the related t-test*. Also, there are the two 'bonus' tests, designed for working out the significance of data from correlational studies – *the Pearson product-moment calculation* and *Spearman's rho*. To ensure you make the appropriate selection, ask yourself some questions about your study and about the data it has produced:

Question 1   What kind of methodology have you used?
If you've done a **correlational study**, skip to **Box 4X**. Otherwise, go to Question 2.

Question 2   What kind of *design* does your study have?
If it has a *repeated measures* or *matched pairs* design select from **Sign test, Wilcoxon test** or **Related t-test**. If it has an *independent* design select from **Chi-square test, Mann–Whitney U-test** or **Unrelated t-test.** Your answer to Question 2 narrows your choice down considerably. Chapter 3 reviews the different types of *design*. Now go to Question 3.

Question 3   What *level of measurement* does your study use?
If it uses the *nominal* level select the **Chi-square test** (for *independent* designs) or the **Sign test** (for *repeated measures* or *matched pairs*

Box 4Q *continued*

designs). If it uses the *ordinal* level, select the **Mann–Whitney U-test** (for *independent* designs) or the **Wilcoxon test** (for *repeated measures* or *matched pairs* designs). If your study uses the *interval* level (the criteria for *interval* status are fairly strict) you may be able to select what's called a **parametric** test. The **Unrelated t-test** and the **Related t-test** are examples of these. **Parametric** tests are regarded as very precise tests of inference, but in order to 'gain access' to them you need to subject your data to the further rigours of Questions 4 and 5.

Question 4 Do the sets of scores from both your conditions approximate *normal distribution*?

If the sets of scores from both your conditions approximate *normal distribution* you're on course for selecting a parametric test. To make a decision on this use an 'eye-ball test' or a 'test of goodness of fit' (these are explained in the section on *normal distribution* in the first half of this chapter). If your answer to Question 4 is 'no', convert your data to the *ordinal* level by putting them into rank order (Appendix 5 has a guide to ranking scores). Then select one of the inferential tests recommended in Question 3, for *ordinal* scores. If your answer to Question 4 is 'yes', go to Question 5.

Question 5 Are the sets of scores from both your conditions *similarly dispersed*?

In other words, are they 'spread out' to a similar extent (the first half of this chapter has a discussion of dispersion)? If your sets are similarly dispersed you're on course for selecting a parametric test. There are two methods for making a decision on 'similarity of dispersion'. First, you can plot your sets on histograms and judge – using an 'eye-ball method' – whether they look like they're similarly spread. This method is usually precise enough. If you're looking for extra precision there's a statistical test specifically designed for measuring 'similarity of dispersion'. It's called the **F-test**. You'll find it in Appendix 6.

If you have *interval* scores and you've answered 'yes' and 'yes' to Questions 4 and 5 respectively, select the **Unrelated t-test for** *independent* designs or the **Related t-test** for *repeated measures* or *matched pairs* designs.

Box 4R   The Sign test

Select this when you have **nominal** data and a **repeated measures** or **matched pairs** design. For example, Terry and Geri contacted ten of their male participants six months after their original study and asked them to rate how scared they were during the original emergency. These second responses were compared with the ones they originally made six months earlier. Terry and Geri used a Sign test to find out if there was a significant difference between the two sets of responses.

Step 1   Arrange the pairs of scores into two columns:

participant	original response	second response	signs
1	'very scared'	'very scared'	
2	not at all	very	–
3	very	not at all	+
4	not at all	a little	–
5	very	a little	+
6	a little	not at all	+
7	a little	not at all	+
8	very	very	
9	a little	a little	
10	not at all	very	–

Step 2   Where the value or magnitude of the first member of a pair exceeds the value of the second, enter a '+' sign in the final column. If the value of the second exceeds that of the first, enter a '–' sign. If the value or magnitude of the pair is equal, leave the fourth column blank.

Step 3   Count the number of times the least frequent sign occurs in the final column to find 's'. The least frequent sign is '–', which occurs 3 times. So S = 3.

Step 4   Total the number of '+' and '–' signs to find N.
There are four '+' signs and three '–' signs. So $N = 7$.

Step 5   Look in the table in Appendix 7 to find out whether the result is significant at the 5% level. In our examples, where $N = 7$, S exceeds 0 for a two-tailed hypothesis, so the result is not significant at the 5% level.

Box 4S The Chi-square test

Select this when you have **nominal** data and an **independent** design. For example, let's say Terry and Geri divided their participants into separate, discrete groups. Those that responded in under 10 seconds and those that didn't. Here's how Terry and Geri would use a Chi-square test to find out if there was a significant difference between the number of males and females in their original study who responded to the emergency in under 10 seconds.

Step 1 Arrange the data in a 2 × 2 table. Call the number in each cell the 'observed' frequency (if your data is more complex and requires, say, a 2 × 3 table, you'll need to use a different form of the Chi-square test – called the Complex chi-square test).

	Column 1(males)	Column 2(females)	Column 3(totals)
row 1 reacted in under 10 secs	cell A 10	cell B 20	30
row 2 reacted in 10 secs or more	cell C 15	cell D 5	20
row 3 totals	25	25	50

Step 2 Calculate the 'expected' frequency for each cell. Do this by multiplying the row total by the column total for each cell, then by dividing the outcome by the overall total. Note than an 'expected' frequency of less than 5 for any cell is regarded as so small as to invalidate the Chi-square test.
cell A: $(30 \times 25) \div 50 = 15$ expected frequency = 15
cell B: $(25 \times 30) \div 50 = 15$ expected frequency = 15
cell C: $(20 \times 25) \div 50 = 10$ expected frequency = 10
cell D: $(20 \times 25) \div 50 = 10$ expected frequency = 10

Step 3 For each cell find the difference between the *observed* and *expected* frequency. Do this by subtracting the smaller value from the larger.
cell A: 15 (expected) − 10 (observed) = 5
cell B: 20 (observed) − 15 (expected) = 5
cell C: 15 (observed) − 10 (expected) = 5
cell D: 10 (expected) − 5 (observed) = 5

Box 4S *continued*

Step 4 Square each of the values from step 3, then divide the outcome by the expected frequency for that cell.
  cell A: $5^2 \div 15 = 1.7$
  cell B: $5^2 \div 15 = 1.7$
  cell C: $5^2 \div 10 = 2.5$
  cell D: $5^2 \div 10 = 2.5$

Step 5 Total the values from step 4 to find χ^2: $1.7 + 1.7 + 2.5 + 2.5 = 8.4$, $\chi^2 = 8.4$

Step 6 Look in the table in Appendix 8 to find out if the result is significant at the 5% level. In our example, χ^2 exceeds 3.841 for a two-tailed hypothesis, so the result is significant at the 5% level.

Box 4T The Wilcoxon test

Select this when you have **ordinal** data and a **repeated measures** or *matched pairs* design. For example, Terry and Geri contacted ten of their male participants six months after their original study and tested their reactions to a similar emergency. They wanted to compare the reaction times in this second trial to those from the original research. To see if there was a significant difference between the two sets of scores they opted for a non-parametric test. The Wilcoxon test was the appropriate choice.

Step 1 Arrange the pairs of scores in two columns:

Participant	Column 1 1st reaction time (in seconds)	Column 2 2nd reaction time (in seconds)	Column 3 difference	Column 4 ranked difference
1	3	3	0	
2	5	1	4	4.5
3	8	2	6	6
4	8	15	−7	7.5
5	8	1	7	7.5
6	11	9	2	3
7	11	7	4	4.5
8	11	10	1	1.5
9	14	14	0	
10	21	22	−1	1.5

Box 4T   *continued*

> **Step 2**   Work out the value for 'difference between each pair' (see column 3 above). Do this by subtracting each value from its pair. For each pair be sure to subtract in the same direction. For example, in the above table the second pair value is always subtracted from the first.
>
> **Step 3**   Rank the 'differences between each pair' values from step 2. Give the smallest difference the rank of 1 (see column 4 above). Whilst ranking the scores, *ignore all positive and negataive signs* and *ignore all scores of zero*. The latter are excluded from this test. Appendix 5 has a guide to ranking scores.
>
> **Step 4**   Add up the ranks for all the 'differences between each pair' that are positive, then add up the ranks for all the 'differences between each pair' that are negative. Let the smaller of these two totals be 'T'. In our example there are only two negative 'differences between each pair'. Their ranks are 1.5 and 7.5, so $T = 9$.
>
> **Step 5**   Look in the table in Appendix 9 to find out if the result is significant at the 5% level. As you do so, be sure to exclude any zero 'differences between each pair' values from N. So in our example, since there are two such zero values, $N = 8$. In our example, I exceeds 4 for a two-tailed hypothesis, so the result is not significant at the 5% level.

Box 4U   The Mann–Whitney U-test

> Select this when you have **ordinal** data and an **independent** design. For example, say Terry and Geri did their original study with 20 participants in each condition. And say their data fell short of the criteria for selecting a parametric test (see **Box 4P**), so they opted for a non-parametric test. The Mann–Whitney test would be the appropriate choice.
>
> **Step 1**   Arrange the scores in columns. If one set has fewer scores, make this *'set A'*. Here are the columns for the example described above. The values in brackets are the rank scores (see step 5).

Box 4U *continued*

Set A (male condition)	Set B (female condition)
4 (5)	1 (1.5)
5 (7)	1 (1.5)
6 (9.5)	3 (3.5)
8 (12.5)	3 (3.5)
9 (14)	5 (7)
10 (15)	5 (7)
11 (16.5)	6 (9.5)
11 (16.5)	7 (11)
14 (18.5)	8 (12.5)
14 (18.5)	18 (20)

Step 2   Count how many scores are in each set to find NA and NB. Multiply NA by NB to find $NANB$. In our example $NA = 10$, $NB = 10$. So $NANB = 100$.

Step 3   Add 1 to NA:
$NA +1 = 11$.

Step 4   Multiply $NA+1$ by NA, then divide the outcome by 2:
$110 \div 2 = 55$.

Step 5   Rank all the scores from both sets, *taken as one set*. Appendix 5 has a guide to ranking scores. Give the smallest score rank 1. In the table in step 1, ranks are shown in brackets.

Step 6   Add up the ranks from the scores in *set A*:
$5 + 7 + 9.5 + 12.5 + 14 + 15 + 16.5 + 16.5 + 18.5 + 18.5 = 133$.

Step 7   Add $NANB$ to the outcome of step 4, then subtract the outcome of step 6.
$100 + 55 - 133 = 22$.

Step 8   Subtract the outcome of step 7 from $NANB$:
$100 - 22 = 78$.

Step 9   Call the outcomes of steps 7 and 8 U and U'. Whichever is smallest is U.
$U = 22$, $U' = 78$.

Step 10   Look in the table in Appendix 10 to see if the result is significant at the 5% level. In our example U does not exceed 23 for a two-tailed hypothesis, so the result is significant at the 5% level.

Box 4V   The Related t-test

Select this when you have **interval scores**, when sets **approximate normal distribution** and are **similarly dispersed** and when you have a **repeated measures** or **matched pairs** design. For example, Terry and Geri contacted 20 of the participants from their follow-up study (see the section on normal distribution for details of this) at a later date and tested their reaction time in a similar emergency. They measured reaction time at the interval level of measurement. Both their sets approximate normal distribution and were similarly dispersed. So the *Related t* was the appropriate test of significance.

Step 1   Arrange the scores in two columns:

part	Set A (reaction time 1)	Set B (reaction time 2)	A–B (step 7)	(A–B)² (step 8)
1	2	1	1	1
2	2	7	−5	25
3	3	2	1	1
4	5	3	2	4
5	6	3	3	9
6	7	4	3	9
7	8	4	4	16
8	8	7	1	1
9	9	7	2	4
10	9	6	3	9
11	10	6	4	16
12	10	6	4	16
13	10	8	2	4
14	11	5	6	36
15	11	8	3	9
16	12	10	2	4
17	12	11	1	1
18	13	9	4	16
19	15	5	10	100
20	16	13	3	9
			Total 54	**Total 290**

Step 2   Count up the pairs to find N: $N = 20$.

Step 3   Calculate $N-1$ to find df: $20-1 = 19$, $df = 19$.

Box 4V   *continued*

Step 4   Multiply the *N* by *df*: 20 × 19 = 380.

Step 5   Find the mean for each set:
Set A: 2 + 2 + 3 + 5 + 6 + 7 + 8 + 8 + 9 + 9 + 10 + 10 + 10
   + 11 + 11 + 12 + 12 + 13 + 15 + 16 = 179
   179 ÷ 20 = 9   *Set A* mean = 9
Set B: 1 + 2 + 3 + 3 + 4 + 4 + 5 + 5 + 6 + 6 + 7+ 7 + 7
   + 8 + 8 + 9 + 10 + 11 + 13 = 125
   125 ÷ 20 = 6.3   *Set B* mean = 6.3

Step 6   Find the 'difference between the means' by subtracting the smaller one from the larger:
9 − 6.3 = 2.7.

Step 7   Subtract each score in *set B* from its pair in *set A*. See the table in step 1 for the outcomes of these calculations.

Step 8   Square the outcome of step 7 for each pair, then add up the squared values. See the table in step 1.
Total of the squared values = 290.

Step 9   Add the differences between each pair from step 7, *taking negative signs into account*. See the table in step1.
Total of the differences between each pair = 54.

Step 10   Square the outcome of step 9, then divide by *N*: $54^2 ÷ 20 = 145.8$.

Step 11   Subtract the outcome of step 10 from the outcome of step 8, then divide by the outcome of step 4.
(290 − 145.8) ÷ 380 = 0.38.

Step 12   Find the square root of the outcome of step 11: $\sqrt{0.38} = 0.62$.

Step 13   Divide the outcome of step 6 by the outcome of step 12 to find *t*: 2.7 ÷ 0.62 = 4.35,   *t* = 4.35.

Step 14   Look in the table in Appendix 11 to see if the result is significant at the 5% level. In our example, *t* exceeds 2.093 for a two-tailed hypothesis, so the result is significant at the 5% level.

Box 4W   The Unrelated t-test

Select this when you have **interval scores**, when your sets **approximate normal distribution** and are **similarly dispersed** and you have an **independent** design. For example, let's say Terry and Geri obtained the data listed below from two separate conditions in an independent design experiment.

Step 1   Arrange the scores in two columns:

participant	Set A	(A^2)	Set B	(B^2)
1	2	4	1	1
2	2	4	7	49
3	3	9	2	4
4	5	25	3	9
5	6	36	3	9
6	7	49	4	16
7	8	64	4	16
8	8	64	7	49
9	9	81	7	49
10	9	81	6	36
11	10	100	6	36
12	10	100	6	36
13	10	100	8	64
14	11	121	5	25
15	11	121	8	64
16	12	144	10	100
17	12	144	11	121
18	13	169	9	81
19	15	225	5	25
20	16	256	13	169
Totals	**179**	**1897**	**125**	**959**

Step 2   Count the number of scores in each set to find NA and NB, then add Ns to Nt to find N: 20 + 20 = 40.
$N = 40$.

Step 3   Multiply NA by NB to find $NANB$, then divide the outcome of step 2 by $NsNt$: 40 ÷ 400 = 0.1.

Step 4   Total the scores in *set A*: set A total = 179.

Step 5   Square all the scores in *set A*, then total all the squares. See the table in step 1.

Box 4W *continued*

Step 6   Square the outcome of step 4, then divide the outcome by
NA: $179^2 \div 20 = 32041 \div 20 = 1602.1$.

Step 7   Subtract the outcome of step 6 from the outcome of step 5:
$1897 - 1602.1 = 294.9$.

Step 8   Total the scores in *set B*: *set B* total $= 125$.

Step 9   Square all the scores in *set B*, then total all the squares. See
the table in step 1.

Step 10   Square the outcome of step 8, then divide the outcome by
NB: $125^2 \div 20 = 15625 \div 20 = 781.3$.

Step 11   Subtract the outcome of step 10 from the outcome of step 9:
$959 - 781.3 = 177.7$.

Step 12   Add the outcome of step 7 to the outcome of step 11: $294.9 + 177.7 = 472.6$.

Step 13   Calculate $N - 2$ to find df (degrees of freedom – this is a
mathematical concept related to the number of observations
that are contained in your data): $40 - 2 = 38$, $df = 38$.

Step 14   Divide the outcome of step 12 by df, then multiply the
outcome by the outcome of step 3: $(472.6/38) \times 0.1 = 1.24$.

Step 15   Find the square root of the outcome of step 14: $\sqrt{1.24} = 1.1$.

Step 16   Find the means of *sets A* and *B*, then subtract the smaller
from the larger.
(*set A* mean is $179 \div 20 = 9$) – (*set B* mean is $125 \div 20 = 6.3$)
$= 2.7$.

Step 17   Divide the outcome of step 16 by the outcome of step 15 to
find t: $2.7 \div 1.1 = 2.5$, $t = 2.5$.

Step 18   Look in the table in Appendix 11 to see if the result is significant
at the 5% level. In our example, t exceeds 2.021 for a two-
tailed hypothesis, so the result is significant at the 5% level.

Box 4X   Three steps to take before calculating correlation co-efficients

Take these steps when you've done a **correlational study**, you have **paired sets of scores** for two variables and you want to find out if the positive or negative correlation between them is significant at the 5 per cent level (see earlier in this chapter for details of this). These three steps will enable you to select the appropriate co-efficient calculation for your data (you have two to choose from and these are featured in **Boxes 4Y** and **4Z**). For the moment, let's use an example to clarify things. Let's say you're correlating 'the number of multiplex cinemas in six towns' (*variable A*) with 'the number of recorded incidents of joyriding in those towns' (*variable B*). And let's say that you predict a positive correlation, where 'number of cinemas' and 'number of incidents' will rise and fall together. Here are your scores:

Town 1	Town 2	Town 3	Town 4	Town 5	Town 6
Variable A (cinemas)					
12	13	14	15	17	18
Variable B (joyriding)					
61	67	70	80	84	88

Step 1   Arrange your two sets of data in a **scattergram**. This is the name given to **a graph for showing the strength of the correlation between two sets of scores**. The vertical axis of a scattergram measures *variable A*, the horizontal axis

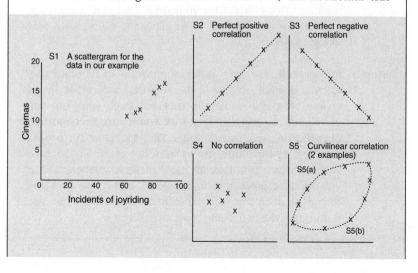

Box 4X *continued*

measures *variable B*. S1 below is a scattergram for the data in our example:

Step 2 Ask yourself 'what kind "shape" does my scattergram have?' Is it most similar to S2, S3, S4 or S5 below?
S2 Perfect positive correlation
S3 Perfect negative correlation
S4 No correlation
S5 Curvilinear correlation

If it's similar to *S2* or *S3*, go to step 3. If it's similar to *S4* it's safe to conclude that your correlation is not significant at the 5 per cent level. There's no correlation between your sets of scores. Quit your calculations here. If your scattergram is similar to *S5* your scores are not really appropriate for either of the two methods for calculating correlation co-efficients (just to qualify this a little: a *slight* curve in your scattergram is permissible if you're using the Spearman's rho [coming up below], though the Pearson product-moment [coming up below] certainly won't tolerate a curved shape in your scattergram (it needs to be 'linear'). A shape like those in *S5* means you've found a 'curvilinear' relationship between your two sets of scores, which is certainly an interesting finding in itself, when it's presented in the form of a scatter-gram. But any further tests of correlation will probably give a misleading co-efficient for your data. Quit your calculations here. As for our example, *S1* is similar to *S2*, so we'll press ahead to step 3.

Step 3 Ask yourself 'what level of measurement does my study use?' There's a guide to 'levels of measurement' earlier in this chapter. If you're using the **interval** level, work out your correlation co-efficient using **Pearson product-moment correlation**, which you'll find in **Box 4Y** below. For **ordinal** data, use **Spearman's rho** to work out your correlation co-efficient, which is in **Box 4Z**. Both these calculations will tell you the significance of your co-efficient at the 5 per cent level, though Pearson's product-moment is regarded as the more powerful of the two, being a parametric test.

Box 4Y   Pearson's product-moment calculation

Select this when you have **paired** sets of scores at the **interval** level of measurement and when the shape of your scattergram approximates *S2* or *S3* in **Box 4X** (in other words, when your scores have a linear, rather than curved, distribution). For our example, we'll use the scores from the 'multiplex cinema' study, which is described in **Box 4X**.

Step 1   Arrange your scores into a table, as follows:

	Column 1 Variable A score	Column 2 A^2	Column 3 Variable B score	Column 4 B^2	Column 5 $A \times B$
Town 1	12	144	61	3,721	732
Town 2	13	169	67	4,489	871
Town 3	14	196	70p	4,900	980
Town 4	15	225	80	6,400	1,200
Town 5	17	289	84	7,056	1,428
Town 6	18	324	88	7,744	1,584
Totals	**89**	**1374**	**450**	**34,310**	**6,795**

Step 2   Count the number of paired sets, to find N: $N = 6$.

Step 3   Calculate *column 2* total × N: $1374 \times 6 = 8244$.

Step 4   Square the *column 1* total: $89^2 = 7921$.

Step 5   Subtract the outcome of step 4 from the outcome of step 3: $8244 - 7921 = 323$.

Step 6   Calculate *column 4* total × N: $34,310 \times 6 = 205,860$.

Step 7   Square the *column 3* total: $450^2 = 202,500$.

Step 8   Subtract the outcome of step 7 from the outcome of step 6: $205,860 - 202,500 = 3360$.

Step 9   Multiply the outcome of step 8 by the outcome of step 5: $3360 \times 323 = 1,085,280$.

Step 10   Find the square root of the outcome of step 9: $\sqrt{1,085,280} = 1041.8$.

Step 11   Multiply the *column 5* total by N: $6795 \times 6 = 40,770$.

Box 4Y *continued*

Step 12 Multiply the *column 1* total by the *column 3* total: 89 × 450 = 40,050.

Step 13 Subtract the outcome of step 12 from the outcome of step 11. Don't worry if the outcome is negative:
40,770 − 40,050 = 720.

Step 14 Divide the outcome of step 13 by the outcome of step 10, to find r: 720 ÷ 1041.8 = 0.7, $r = 0.7$.

Step 15 Look in the table in Appendix 12 to see if the result is significant at the 5% level. In our example, r is less than 0.729 for a one-tailed hypothesis, so the result is not significant at the 5% level.

Box 4Z Spearman's rho calculation for working out correlation co-efficients

Select this when you have **paired** sets of scores at the **ordinal** level of measurement and when the shape of your scattergram approximates $S2$ or $S3$ in **Box 4X** (in other words, when your scores have a linear, rather than curved, distribution). For our example we'll use the rank values of the scores from a study in which 'the number of multiplex cinemas in each of six towns' (*variable A*) is correlated with 'the number of points that town's biggest men's football team has amassed in the present season' (*variable B*).

Step 1 Arrange your scores into a table, as follows:

	Column 1 Variable A score	Column 2 Variable B score	Column 3 Rank A	Column 4 Rank B	Column 5 Rank A− Rank B	Column 6 (Rank A− Rank B)^2
Town 1	12	61	1	6	−5	25
Town 2	13	58	2	5	−3	9
Town 3	14	53	3	3.5	−0.5	0.25
Town 4	15	53	4	3.5	0.5	0.25
Town 5	17	50	5	2	3	9
Town 6	18	1	6	1	5	25
						Total 68.5

Box 4Z   *continued*

Step 2   Count the number of paired sets, to find N: $N = 6$.

Step 3   Calculate $(N \times N \times N) - N$: $(6 \times 6 \times 6) - 6 = 210$.

Step 4   Multiply the *column 6* total by 6: $68.5 \times 6 = 411$.

Step 5   Divide the outcome of step 4 by the outcome of step 3: $411 \div 210 = 1.96$.

Step 6   Subtract the outcome of step 5 from 1 to find rho: $1 - 1.96 = -0.96$, rho $= -0.96$.

Step 7   Look in the table in Appendix 13 to see if the result is significant at the 5% level. In our example, rho exceeds 0.886 for a two-tailed hypothesis, so the result is significant at the 5% level.

Bonus Box   Using Inferential Statistics: A–Z of terms to remember

Inferential statistics demonstrate that a change in the value of a dependent variable can be confidently attributed to a change in the value of an independent variable, rather than to chance, random variation.

Inferential tests enable you to *infer*, from the data you've collected in your study, whether or not your results are significant at the 5 per cent level.

Interval data is presented as scores on a scale with equal units.

Levels of measurement (**interval, ordinal** and **nominal**) are different ways of quantifying behaviour and presenting research data.

Nominal data is presented in separate, discrete groups.

Null hypotheses are predictions of no difference between two sets of scores on a particular variable.

One-tailed hypotheses specify the direction in which an *IV* will influence a *DV*.

Ordinal data is presented in rank order.

Bonus Box *continued*

> **Research hypothesis** predicts a difference between two sets of scores on a particular variable.
>
> **The 5 per cent significance level** is a *set* 'level of doubt' that researchers conventionally operate at when they reject null hypotheses.
>
> **Two-tailed hypotheses** predict that an *IV* will influence a *DV*, but the direction of influence is left unspecified.
>
> **Type one errors** are made when a researcher rejects null hypotheses that should be accepted.
>
> **Type two errors** are made when a researcher accepts null hypotheses that should be rejected.

Now you've dabbled in descriptive and inferential statistics and rejected or accepted your null hypothesis, go ahead and complete your *research report*. Chapter 3 has a guide to *writing research reports*.

▶ The last word

After reading this chapter you should have a clearer idea about why psychological researchers are interested in statistics. Furthermore, you should be able to explain to your family, friends and neighbours that psychologists are interested in *two different kinds of statistics* that do *two different jobs*.

Firstly, **descriptive statistics** reduce large amounts of data to smaller, more manageable helpings. Secondly, **inferential statistics** tell researchers whether their findings are *significant* or not.

5 Studying Psychology in Your Own Preferred Learning Style

Look around your psychology class. You'll see people with quite a bit in common and with plenty to distinguish them as individuals: different tastes in clothes, books, films and crisps; different social and emotional needs. And, most importantly for this chapter, they'll all have different styles of learning. Each individual will have their own preferences and needs when it comes to how they learn most effectively. Some like lectures. Some like discussions. Some like playing games.

This final chapter will help you identify your own style of learning and suggest some ways to use that knowledge to become more effective when studying psychology.

Restaurant Utopia

Students and tutors at our college could learn a lot from Frank. Frank runs the restaurant on the first floor. He puts on a lovely spread. More importantly, he puts on a different spread for different people. When you enrol at our college Frank gives you a form to fill in, asking for details of the kind of foods you prefer, the kind of nutrients you're lacking, what you try to avoid for religious, ethical and medical reasons and so on. Frank takes the completed forms away and devises a 'diet profile' for every one of his customers, guaranteeing that every meal you eat at **Restaurant Utopia** will combine 'a little bit of what you fancy' with 'a little bit of what does you good'. The result? Happy, healthy students and tutors. If only they themselves would apply Frank's motto – 'different people like and need different things' – to their own studying and teaching, there really would be a few improvements around here.

Not everyone studies psychology (or anything, for that matter) in the same way. We each have a different **style of learning**. Partly because we all have **individual *preferences* for learning in certain ways** and partly because we all have **individual *needs* that have to be attended to when we're taking in new material**. Some of us *prefer* to be told what to study and how to go about it. Others *prefer* to develop our own pathways through our learning. Some of us *need* silence to be able to concentrate. Others *need* some background noise. No two learners are quite the same. Just like eating at Frank's place, when we're learning we're happiest and most effective when we're combining *a little bit of what we fancy* with *a little bit of what does us good.*

Though this sounds like common sense, it isn't *very* common for tutors and students to pay much attention to individual *styles of learning*. Take tutors, for example. Few of them spend time exploring students' individual learning *needs* and *preferences* with a view to altering their teaching methods to cater for everyone. In their defence, we should say that perhaps this is because of the sheer size of their classes. And so if tutors haven't the time to read every single student's 'learning fingerprint', maybe it's up to students themselves to take matters into their own hands. Yes, that means you. This chapter offers you a guide to identifying your own individual *needs* and *preferences*, so you can devise your own *learning profile* and answer questions such as: *What kind of psychology student am I? Why do I excel in some areas of my course and not others? Could I prepare for assessments more effectively?* Furnished with answers to these questions, your performance ought to improve, however good it already is.

Before proceeding any further, though, let's take a swift look at how three sets of researchers have tried to complete the sentence *Different people have different styles of learning in terms of . . .*

• Dunn and Dunn (1986) suggest that *Different people have different styles of learning in terms of how they concentrate when learning new material and skills.* A key influence here is **the learning environment**. To be more specific, different levels of sound, light and temperature suit different people, as does the chair they choose to sit in. For example, you may work best with some background noise to block out the noise of your own breathing or rustling papers. Alternatively, you may work well with subdued lighting. Or you may prefer to lounge on the floor rather than sit at a table. It's a matter of personal style. There's no one right way.

* Mumford (1993) says: *Different people have different styles of learning in terms of how they acquire new skills and information.* For them, learning takes place at different stages of a *learning cycle.* This cycle incorporates a number of processes that are ongoing during all kinds of learning. Processes such as *reflection, planning, experiencing.* For Mumford, **different people learn most effectively at different stages of the learning cycle.** Some of us are by nature *reflectors* who like to stand back, observe and stroke our chins as we learn. Others are *activists,* best employed when engrossed in 'here and now' activities. A third group, *pragmatists,* like to be shown how something is done according to an established model. Fourthly, *theorists* are happy to acquire abstract ideas that have no immediately obvious practical application. Whilst some people are in the happy position of being able to thrive at more than one stage of the learning cycle, no single style is superior to any other – though you could argue that some courses attract people who thrive at particular stages of the learning cycle, for example, pure maths might attract *theorists.*

* Sadler-Smith (1996) says *Different people have different styles of learning in terms of the kind of learning activities they prefer to take part in.* This relates to **how much power and influence we have over our learning.** Some of us are *dependent learners* who like tutors to give us instructions in structured scenarios like lectures and seminars, preferably with deadlines imposed. Some of us are *independent* learners who like to exert some influence over (and negotiate with our tutor) the options we take, the assignments we do. Here, the tutor is seen as a resource to be used, not an authority whose word is taken as law. Thirdly, *collaborative* learners are social animals who work best on group projects. All three of these styles of learning can be effective, although they're not all equally catered for in the typical college setting.

You'd be right to conclude from these three models that plenty has been said and written about *individual styles of learning.* In fact, there are shelvesful of research on the subject. To narrow things down a little, the rest of this chapter will focus on two models that have plenty to offer undergraduate psychologists who want to find out more about the strengths and weaknesses of their own learning, about how to make the most of their strengths and about how to iron out their weaknesses. With all this in mind, from time to time over the next few pages you'll be encouraged to take **three significant steps towards being better at studying psychology**:

- **Step 1 Know your profile** – find out your individual style of learning.

- **Step 2 Play to your strengths** – organise your learning to make the most of areas you excel in.

- **Step 3 Chip away at your weaknesses** – organise your learning to improve in areas you don't excel in.

▷ Wholist and analytic learners

When you describe a film you saw the previous day to your mother or your neighbour do you find yourself remembering the *grand themes* or the *minutiae*? Do you dwell on the overall feel of the film – what film students call its *mise-en-scène* – or do you come up with accurate – yet often disjointed – details, word-for-word one-liners and intricate plot details? Which are you, the 'big picture' film critic or the stickler for 'fine detail'? If you're the former, chances are you're what Eugene Sadler-Smith (1996) has called a *wholist learner*. If you're the latter, you may be one of Sadler-Smith's *analytic learners*.

The difference between the two refers to how we organise and process new material. In effect, we're talking about two styles of thinking. *Wholist learners* excel at learning and remembering the big themes in new material. They prioritise these at the expense of the 'small change' of detail and factual accuracy, both of which they're happy to sort out later or ignore altogether. For the *analytic learner*, fine detail is top priority. They're happiest concentrating on analysing facts, rather than considering global themes. Indeed, an overall understanding of major themes rarely dawns on *analytics* until all the facts and details have been accumulated. You could say *wholist learners* think 'top–down', *analytics* think 'bottom–up'.

Know your profile: wholist or analytic?
You may already have a pretty shrewd idea of which of these thinking styles is most applicable to you. If not, or if you're on the lookout for confirmation, here is a method for sorting out the wholists from the analytics.

The 'Milgram Memory' text

Try the test in **Box 5A**, which is based on Milgram's obedience experiment.

Did you find **set A** or **set B** more challenging? If you struggled more with **set A** but faired reasonably well on **set B** there's a good chance you're an *analytic* learner. If it was the other way around you may well be a *wholist* learner.

The *Milgram memory test* will give you some indication of the *strengths* and *weaknesses* of your thinking style. If you want to try a more rigorous *wholist–analytic* test, have a look at Riding's *Cognitive Styles Analysis* (1991).

Play to your strengths: wholist or analytic?

Knowing whether you tend towards the *wholist* or *analytic* style of thinking should help you explain a few things. Knowing how you process new material should help you work out why you excel in some areas of your psychology course and not others.

Box 5A The Milgram memory test

Base your responses to this test on what you know about Milgram's experiment on obedience (1963). If you're already familiar with the study, go ahead and answer the questions in **sets A** and **B** below. If not, read the summary in Chapter 1, then try the questions.

Set A
- What's the rationale for this study?
- What's the use of this study to society as a whole?
- Write down one similarity between Milgram's study and any other piece of research.
- Suggest four problems with this kind of research.

Set B
- How did Milgram get his sample?
- What was the 'learner's' surname?
- What percentage of participants obeyed to the maximum voltage in the original study?
- Name the four variables Milgram manipulated in his follow-up studies.

Wholist learners tend to excel at ...
- grasping the aims and rationales of studies and theories.
- identifying links between pieces of research.
- identifying the paradigms (schools of thought) pieces of research are drawn from (Chapter 1 has more on paradigms).
- identifying similarities between pieces of research.
- understanding links between testable statements and the theories they're drawn from (Chapter 1 has more on statements and theories).
- identifying the usefulness of research to society as a whole.

Analytic learners tend to excel at ...
- recalling procedural details of research.
- recognising important design and control features of studies.
- summarising and identifying important findings from studies.
- identifying weaknesses in research.
- recalling names and dates associated with research.

Chip away at your weaknesses: wholist or analytic?
Riding and Cheemal (1991) suggest that once you know which thinking style you prefer you should focus on the *other* one – the one you like least. I call this *the jugglers' method of learning to learn*, based on the well-known circus maxim that jugglers devote most of their practice time to training their subordinate hand (Finnigan 1992) to the standard of their superior hand. What we're talking about here is a *balanced* approach to learning new material – a flexible style of thinking that enables you to process material efficiently whether it comes to you in the form of 'the big global themes' or the 'flotsam and jetsam of factual detail'. A logical step towards achieving this balance is to **organise your learning in a way that compensates for your weaker, least preferred style of thinking**. So *wholists*, be more *analytic*. And *analytics*, vice versa. Here are some practical suggestions:

Wholists, be more analytic by ...
- organising your **note taking** by setting out topics and research in ways that highlight the component parts and substantive facts of the material – drawing attention to them like this will make you less likely to gloss over them.
- adopting an approach to **essay writing** that's 'grounded in detail'. Habitually illustrate your arguments and conclusions with supporting facts, figures, findings and other relevant details.

- testing yourself on the little facts from the relevant research when you're **preparing for assessments**.
- drawing attention to the **differences** between different pieces of research.

Analytics, be more wholist by . . .

- organising your **note taking** in a way that highlights the overall aims and rationales of research. Habitually indicate how research is useful for society as a whole.
- drawing attention to the **similarities** between different pieces of research.
- being aware of **the thinking style of your tutors**, since this may influence the way your class notes are organised. It's worth knowing that the teaching profession tends to attract analytics (Carbo *et al.*, 1986), so it may be that you've been attending classes in which global themes were somewhat neglected. With this in mind, you may want to rewrite your notes in a way that redresses this bias. Let your tutors know what you're doing and why you're doing it. They might be glad of the feedback on their teaching style.
- adopting an **essay-writing style** that draws out the big themes in the research you're discussing (aims, rationales and applications to society as a whole). Habitually keep in mind the overall requirements of the essay question as you're writing (Chapter 2 is a guide to writing psychology essays).
- testing yourself on the aims, rationales and usefulness of the relevant research when you're **revising for assessments**.

Neither of these two styles of thinking is superior to the other. *Wholist* learning and *analytic* learning both have their strengths. But the most effective, most desirable style of all is one that's well-balanced – part *wholist*, part *analytical*. So think like a juggler. Make the most of what you *do* excel at, develop what you *don't* excel at.

▶ Auditory, visual and tactile-kinaesthetic learners

Are you any good at recalling details from news stories? Your answer to this will probably be 'it depends'. And let's face it, it depends on many factors. One of these will be *how you came across the story to begin with.* In other words, *how the story reached you.* Did someone tell you it? Did you see the pictures on television? Were you physically there, taking part, peripherally or otherwise, in the event that later became news?

According to Marie Carbo and Kenneth and Rita Dunn (1986), some of us excel at remembering material we hear, others do better with stories we see pictures of, others excel when we're physically, actively, involved in what we're trying to learn and remember. You could say it's a matter of *perceptual preference.* If you prefer *learning by hearing* about new material you may be what Carbo, Dunn and Dunn call an *auditory* learner. If *learning by looking* at pictures, images and dramatisations helps you remember, you show signs of being a *visual* learner. If *learning by feeling, making and doing* is your preference, you're probably a *tactile-kinaesthetic* learner. This last group typically includes 'tinkerers' and 'doodlers' who like their learning to involve some kind of activity that has them moving around, making or manipulating objects, working with different textures.

Being a member of any of these groups doesn't mean you learn using one modality *exclusively.* Rather, you flit between the three but maintain a *preference* for one modality in particular. And although these three *perceptual preferences* are all as effective as each other, it seems fairly clear that not all of them are catered for equally well on most undergraduate courses.

Know your profile: auditory, visual or tactile-kinaesthetic?
Try these two methods for separating 'lookers' from 'listeners' and 'manipulators'.

Method 1   the 'figure of speech' test
Try the test in **Box 5B**.

Your two-minute speech may be littered with figures of speech similar to those in all three groups, but it's likely that one group will feature most prominently. If **group A**-type statements loom large in your speech you may well be a *visual* learner. If you use phrases from **group B**, it sounds to me like you're an *auditory* learner. If you lean towards **group C** it feels like you're a *visual-kinaesthetic* learner.

Method 2   the 'who are you most like?' test
Now try the test in **Box 5C**.

Box 5B The 'figure of speech' test

Select a piece of psychological research you're familiar with. I'm using Freud's case of Little Hans as an example. If you're not familiar with the research, see Chapter 1 for a full description. To take the test, cover up the three boxes below. Next, talk about your selected piece of research for two minutes. Record your speech onto audio tape. Play it back and note down any 'figures of speech' that are similar to those in **groups A**, **B** or **C**.

Group A	**Group B**	**Group C**
'. . . from Freud's point of view . . . looking at the case of Hans . . . from the psychoanalytic perspective . . . the problem with this study is clear to see . . . the way I see it . . . a confused picture of a phobia emerges . . . an intimate portrait . . .'	'. . . this theory sounds convincing. . . . Freud only heard what he wanted to hear. . . . Hans's plea fell on deaf ears . . . listening to Hans's case . . . to Freud, Hans's symptoms sounded like a phobia. . . . Freud never heard Hans talk directly about his father. . . . I've seldom heard such nonsense . . .'	'. . . Freud wrestled with the facts. . . . Freud manipulated the facts . . . a case of square pegs and round holes. . . . I don't feel convinced by his argument . . . a cumbersome approach . . . putting myself in his shoes. . . . Freud paved the way for future research . . .'

If Maurice sounds like you, chances are you're a *visual* learner. If you're more of a Robin, you could be an *auditory* learner. If you're a Barry you probably have a perceptual preference for *tactile-kinaesthetic* learning.

The *figure of speech* and *who are you most* like? *tests* will tell you something about your *perceptual preference*. For another test of *perceptual preference* – straight from the horses' mouths – have a look at Dunn et al.'s *Learning Style Inventory* (1985).

Box 5C The 'who are you most like?' test

**Here are three people talking about themselves:
who are you most like?**

'My name is Maurice and my favourite party game is *Pictionary*. When I'm trying to spell a word I picture it in my head. I've a good memory for faces, but not names. When I'm studying I get distracted by people moving about in my visual field. At weekends I like to watch TV and go to the cinema. I'd rather visit an art gallery than a concert hall or a gym. In psychology classes I always take note of diagrams, demonstrations and slides.'

'I'm Robin and my favourite party game is *Chinese whispers*. When I'm trying to spell a word I say each letter in my head until it sounds right. I'm good at remembering names, but not faces. When I'm reading I get distracted by background noise. In my spare time I enjoy listening to music and chatting on the 'phone. I'd rather visit a concert hall than an art gallery or a gym. I enjoy the lectures on this psychology course and appreciate good, clear verbal explanations.'

'Hi, they call me Barry. My favourite party game is *charades*. When I'm trying to spell a word I write it down. I've a good memory for things I've done and places I've been, though faces and names often escape me. When I'm reading I can't concentrate properly unless I'm physically comfortable. On my days off I enjoy playing sport, cooking, mending and building things. Maurice says I'm a bit of a "tinkerer". I'd rather visit a gym than an art gallery or a concert hall. In psychology classes I like designing research, playing games, going on visits, doing role-plays.'

Play to your strengths: visual, auditory or tactile-kinaesthetic

Knowing your *perceptual preference* should help you explain why you excel in certain areas of your psychology course. It should also help you change the way you learn new material and prepare yourself for assessments to exploit your own individual style. Here are some suggestions.

1 **Visual learners: play to your strengths by** paying special attention to *what your **notes** look like*. With your preference for the visual modality no doubt you already take care with your presentational style, but you could take things further by using *patterned notes*. This involves making 'spidergram pictures' to illustrate *central* and *peripheral* themes from concepts, studies or theories (or whatever it is you're making notes on). *Patterning* is fully explained in Chapter 2 in the section on essay planning.

Making written text into patterns and pictures plays into the hands of *visual* learners. Try to do this whenever you **plan and prepare for assignments**. Why is it so effective? Because it exploits your natural preference for *thinking and remembering in images*. **Box 5D** shows a typical example of a visual learner's notes. She's illustrated some positive and negative evaluations of Freud's case of Little Hans by using cartoons that help her remember them. As you'll know if you're one yourself, *visual* learners are often picture-junkies. Their notes are littered with diagrams, spidergrams, pie charts and cartoons. To an outsider it may look a bit batty, but it's actually a smart attempt to make the most of a particular style of learning.

One last thought for visual learners. Ask your tutor to recommend **readings** for topics *in advance* of class. You'll respond better to the material if you're introduced to it by *seeing* it first, rather than by *hearing* about it in a lecture (Carbo *et al.*, 1986).

2 **Auditory learners: play to your strengths by** finding a cassette recorder. To some people these are outmoded machines, trapped in the 1970s along with three-bar fires. To you they're a valuable learning aid. In fact, you're a bit of a human cassette recorder yourself. You probably recall a far higher percentage of what your hear in **lectures** than learners with other styles do (Carbo *et al.*, 1986) – much of it word for word. A good set of written **notes** will cement your understanding further. And this is where your cassette recorder comes in. As you **prepare for assessments** supplement your regular revision methods by recording the key points from the material you're revising onto a tape, then playing it back to yourself regularly in the run-up to the big day (or night). Your memory for the material will be reinforced in precisely the way that suits your perceptual preference.

Another way of turning audio-cassette technology to your advantage

Box 5D   Evaluating Freud's Little Hans study using words and pictures

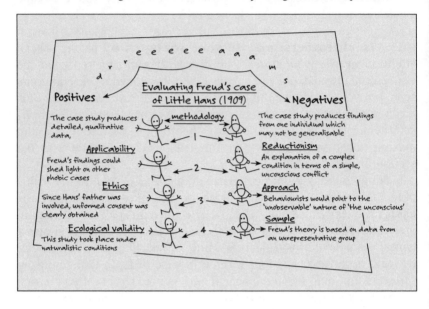

is to record the **lectures** you attend, again playing them back later to reinforce your understanding. To avoid embarrassing scenes, ask permission first. I'd guess that most lecturers, far from being unnerved by the idea, will probably be flattered. Although these recordings won't *replace* your written notes, they'll make a handy complement.

Unlike *visual* learners, auditory learners benefit from doing the **readings** for topics *after* lectures or classes. This way, new material is introduced through the auditory modality first. Your readings will have the greatest impact if you use them as a follow-up to what you've already heard.

3   Tactile-kinaesthetic learners: play to your strengths by *feeling* your way through your course wherever you can. Your style of learning is often undervalued in undergraduate teaching, where the learner's role is traditionally seen as a *passive* one. But being aware of your preference for *feeling, making and doing* will help explain why you find yourself twiddling your thumbs and doodling during talks and lectures. And whilst you'll have little influence over the proportion of *activity-based* classes that crop up on your psychology course, there are some steps you can take to make your learning more *tactile-kinaesthetic friendly*.

Firstly, you can recognise and make the most of the *feeling, making and doing* activities that *do* figure on psychology courses – **designing and carrying out research, seminar presentations** and **role-plays**. Expect to excel on these activities.

As for **lectures**, rather than regarding them as 'one-way learning traffic' where *they talk and you listen*, focus on the one thing you can have an influence over – the quality of your written notes.

When **preparing for essays and timed assignments** you have several opportunities to take matters into your own hands. Don your inventor's hat. Make up games and devices to reinforce your learning. I've outlined two *activities for feeling, making and doing psychology* in **Boxes 5E** and **5F**. Both require cardboard, *Post-it* notes, glue and laminating facilities, so make friends with your college stationer. These games and devices are designed to improve your learning *as you make and use them*, so invest some time researching and designing them. See it as a craft, rather than a chore. These activities can be adapted to use on your own or with other learners. You could even suggest them to your tutor as potential class activities.

The *Post-it board* and *Top Psychology Trumps* both aim to make preparing for psychology assessments and learning about research more of a *tactile-kinaesthetic friendly* activity than, say, reading and writing notes.

Speaking from personal experience as a tutor, I've found they make lively and useful class activities. Methods like these won't replace your

Box 5E   Activities for feeling, making and doing psychology (1)

The *Post-it* Evaluation Board

Cut out a circular card to a size that suits. Divide the circle into either 14 or 7 segments. In the former case, write the name of an evaluation issue from 'the DRREEEEEAAAMSS system for evaluating studies' (this features in Chapter 2) in each of the 14 segments. In the latter, write the name of an evaluation issue for evaluating theories (also in Chapter 2). In the middle of the circle leave a blank space. Now you've made your 'evaluation board'. (You could laminate it, for a wipe-clean finish.)

Now write the name of a study or theory on a *Post-it*. Stick this in the middle of your circle. Think of as many positive and negative evaluations as you can for that study or theory. Explain each evaluation on a separate *Post-it*. Now stick your evaluations in the appropriate segment on

Box 5E   *continued*

your evaluation board. You could have different colours for positive and negative respectively.

The *Post-it* board is a good way of formulating detailed evaluations for research. Use it individually or in groups. Attach a coat hanger to the back of your evaluation board and hang it where your brother's dart board used to be, for easy access.

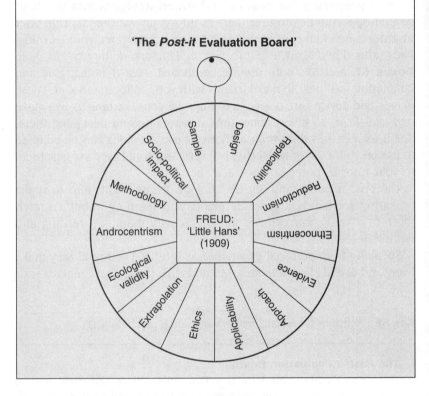

'The *Post-it* Evaluation Board'

more traditional preparation methods, though they can be a welcome change for doodlers. Use them at your convenience. Better still, make up your own. Other 'touchy-feely' activities might include:

- asking each member of your group to bring in an object or prop to introduce a piece of research;
- 'psychology charades' using 'classic studies' instead of books, films and so forth;

Box 5F   Activities for feeling, making and doing psychology (2)

'Top psychology trumps'

Make a deck of cards with a different card for each study you've covered on your course. On each card include: (a) the researcher's name and the date of the study, (b) the title, (c) a short outline of the procedure and findings and (d) a rating of 1–5 (compiled by you, awarding a maximum '5' for a good rating, a minimum '1' for a poor rating) for some appropriate evaluation issues from 'the DRREEEEEAAAMSS system for evaluating studies' (see Chapter 2). Laminate your cards for a stronger finish.

Now you have your deck you can carry it with you everywhere and flick through the cards on the bus, in queues and at other opportune moments. Alternatively, you can play 'top trumps'. This is a game for two players. First, deal the cards evenly between the players. Player 1 then describes the study on her 'top card' and selects one evaluation issue. She reads out the 1–5 rating for that evaluation issue, for that particular study. If this value is greater than the corresponding value on Player 2's top card, Player 2 must surrender his top card to Player 1, who then places both cards at the bottom of her deck. Player 1 then repeats the sequence by reading from her next 'top card'. This goes on – sometimes for days – until one player has no cards left.

Malgram (1963)	Freud (1909)	Festinger and Carlsmith (1959)
'Obedience Experiment'	'Little Hans'	'Forced compliance'
procedure ～～～～ and ～～～～ results ～～～～	procedure ～～～～ and ～～～～ results ～～～～	procedure ～～～～ and ～～～～ results ～～～～
d ～～ → 3	d ～～ → 1	d ～～ → 4
r ～～ → 4	r ～～ → 1	r ～～ → 4
r ～～ → 3	r ～～ → 1	r ～～ → 1
e ～～ → 2	e ～～ → 1	e ～～ → 3
e ～～ → 1	e ～～ → 3	e ～～ → 3
e ～～ → –	e ～～ → –	e ～～ → –
e ～～ → 3	e ～～ → 3	e ～～ → 1
e ～～ → 1	e ～～ → 3	e ～～ → 3
a ～～ → 5	a ～～ → 3	a ～～ → 3
a ～～ → 5	a ～～ → 4	a ～～ → 5
a ～～ → 3	a ～～ → 1	a ～～ → 3
m ～～ → 3	m ～～ → 3	m ～～ → 3
s ～～ → 4	s ～～ → 1	s ～～ → 2
s ～～ → 4	s ～～ → 1	s ～～ → 2

- psychology blockbusters;
- psychology *Pictionary* and so on.

By the way, many of these activities will also appeal to *visual* learners.

Chip away at your weaknesses: visual, auditory or tactile-kinaesthetic

Whilst all of us have a *perceptual preference* for learning and reinforcing new material, a *balanced* style of learning remains the most desirable one of all. So although it's wise to emphasise your *preferred* modality as you learn, it's also wise to reinforce your learning by dabbling in a wide variety of the methods that feature in this section. Effective learning should have a lot in common with eating at Restaurant Utopia, where a balanced diet of *a little bit of what you fancy* combines nicely with *a little bit of what does you good*. The result? Happy, healthy diners and *satisfied* learners.

▶ The last word

Plenty of psychological research suggests that what we do and think is influenced by what those in the same room as us are doing and thinking. Certainly, there's a lot of truth in this. Nevertheless, when you're learning it may be that you *prefer* and *need* to do things in *your own particular way*. It may be that what the person who's sitting next to you does wouldn't work so well for you, given your own style of learning.

Use this chapter to find out what makes you a different kind of learner from those around you. And when you've done that, work out how you can train yourself to become a more effective *all-round* learner, one who's flexible enough to adapt to circumstances that tend not to stay the same for very long.

Appendix 1   Other methods used in psychology

Longitudinal research

This involves taking a sample of participants and studying them over a long period. This is a form of 'repeated measures' research, in which recordings of the same variables are likely to be made repeatedly. A mixture of qualitative or quantitative methods can be used. Longitudinal research assesses the effect of time on the development of participants.

For example, Hodges and Tizard's *Social and Family Relationships of Ex-institutional Adolescents* (1989).* Here, researchers report on the progress of a sample sixteen-year-olds who had experienced institutional care in their early years. Qualitative and quantitative assessments were made of their relationships with peers, parents, teachers, etc.

Research using non-humans

This involves studying non-humans, usually over a long period, either in their natural environment (often called the 'ethological method') or under controlled conditions. Controlled studies can take the form of experiments or observations, producing a mixture of quantitative and qualitative data. Insights gained from this research can then be extrapolated to humans.

For example, Gardner and Gardner's *Teaching Sign Language to a Chimpanzee* (1969).* Here, Washoe the chimp is taught to communicate via American Sign Language in an attempt to compare the way chimps and human children learn and use language.

Cross-cultural research

This involves comparing elements of two or more cultures or communities in terms of one variable. This may involve one researcher collecting data in their own

For example, Deregowski's *Pictorial Perception and Culture,* (1972).* Here, a number of studies are reviewed, in which preferences for visual art

and an 'other' culture. Or it may involve two (indigenous) researchers collecting data from their own cultures, then collaborating in interpreting the data. Either way, the aim is to examine the effect of cultural factors on a particular behaviour or variable. This method can combine a quantitative and qualitative approach.

are compared across a number of African communities to see if there are culturally universal agreed standards of what is aesthetically pleasing.

---

* All cited and described in P. Banyard and A. Grayson, *Introducing Psychological Research* (Basingstoke: Macmillan – now Palgrave, 1996).

Appendix 2   Random number table

To find **random numbers** use this table.

```
19 90 70 99 00 20 21 14 68 86 14 52 41 52 48 87 63 93 95 17 11 29 01 95 80
65 97 38 20 46 85 43 01 72 73 03 37 18 39 11 08 61 74 51 69 89 74 39 82 15
51 67 11 52 49 59 97 50 99 52 18 16 36 78 86 08 52 85 08 40 87 80 61 65 31
17 95 70 45 80 72 68 49 29 31 56 80 30 19 44 89 85 84 46 06 59 73 19 85 23
63 52 52 01 41 88 02 84 27 83 78 35 34 08 72 42 29 72 23 19 66 56 45 65 79
60 61 97 22 61 49 64 92 85 44 01 64 18 39 96 16 40 12 89 88 50 14 49 81 06
98 99 46 50 47 12 83 11 41 16 63 14 52 32 52 25 58 19 68 70 77 02 54 00 52
76 38 03 29 63 79 44 61 40 15 86 63 59 80 02 14 53 40 65 39 27 31 58 50 28
53 05 70 53 30 38 30 06 38 21 01 47 59 38 00 14 47 47 07 26 54 96 87 53 32
02 87 40 41 45 47 24 49 57 74 22 13 88 83 34 32 25 43 62 17 10 97 11 69 84
35 14 97 35 33 68 95 23 92 35 56 54 29 56 93 87 02 22 57 51 61 09 43 95 06
94 51 33 41 67 13 79 93 37 55 14 44 99 81 07 39 77 32 77 09 85 52 05 30 62
91 51 80 32 44 09 61 87 25 21 13 80 55 62 54 28 06 24 25 93 16 71 13 59 78
65 09 29 75 63 20 44 90 32 64 53 89 74 60 41 97 67 63 99 61 46 38 03 93 22
20 71 53 20 25 73 37 32 04 05 56 07 93 89 30 69 30 16 09 05 88 69 58 28 99
01 82 77 45 12 07 10 63 76 35 19 48 56 27 44 87 03 04 79 88 08 13 13 85 51
53 43 37 15 26 92 38 70 96 92 82 11 08 95 97 52 06 79 79 45 82 63 18 27 44
11 39 03 34 25 99 53 93 61 28 88 12 57 21 77 52 70 05 48 34 56 65 05 61 86
40 36 40 96 76 93 86 52 77 65 99 82 93 24 98 15 33 59 05 28 22 87 26 07 47
99 63 22 32 98 18 46 23 34 27 43 11 71 99 31 85 13 99 24 44 49 18 09 79 49
58 24 82 03 47 24 53 63 94 09 74 54 13 26 94 41 10 76 47 91 44 04 95 49 66
47 83 51 62 74 22 06 34 72 52 04 32 92 08 09 82 21 15 65 20 33 29 94 71 11
23 05 47 47 25 07 16 39 33 66 18 55 63 77 09 98 56 10 56 79 77 21 30 27 12
69 81 21 99 21 29 70 83 63 51 70 47 14 54 36 99 74 20 52 36 87 09 41 15 09
35 07 44 75 47 57 90 12 02 07 54 96 09 11 06 23 47 37 17 31 54 08 01 88 63
55 34 57 72 69 33 35 72 67 47 82 80 84 25 39 77 34 55 45 70 08 18 27 38 90
69 66 92 19 09 49 41 31 06 70 05 98 90 07 35 42 38 06 45 18 64 84 73 31 65
90 92 10 70 80 65 19 69 02 83 67 72 16 42 79 60 75 86 90 68 24 64 19 35 51
86 96 98 29 06 92 09 84 38 76 63 49 30 21 30 22 00 27 69 85 29 81 94 78 70
74 16 32 23 02 98 77 87 68 07 66 39 67 98 60 91 51 67 62 44 40 98 05 93 78
39 60 04 59 81 00 41 86 79 79 47 53 53 38 09 68 47 22 00 20 35 55 31 51 51
15 91 29 12 03 57 99 99 90 37 75 91 12 81 19 36 63 32 08 58 37 40 13 68 97
90 49 22 23 62 12 59 52 57 02 55 65 79 78 07 22 07 90 47 03 28 14 11 30 79
98 60 16 03 03 31 51 10 96 46 54 34 81 85 35 92 06 88 07 77 56 11 50 81 69
39 41 88 92 10 96 11 83 44 80 03 92 18 66 75 34 68 35 48 77 33 42 40 90 60
16 95 86 70 75 85 47 04 66 08 00 83 26 91 03 34 72 57 59 13 82 43 80 46 15
52 53 37 97 15 72 82 32 99 90 06 66 24 12 27 63 95 73 76 63 89 73 44 99 05
56 61 87 39 12 91 36 74 43 53 13 29 54 19 28 30 82 13 54 00 78 45 63 98 35
21 94 47 90 12 77 53 84 46 47 85 72 13 49 21 31 91 18 95 58 24 16 74 11 53
23 32 65 41 18 37 27 47 39 19 65 65 80 39 07 84 83 70 07 48 53 21 40 06 71
00 83 63 22 55 34 18 04 52 35 99 01 30 98 64 56 27 09 24 86 61 85 53 83 45
87 64 81 07 83 11 20 99 45 18 45 76 08 64 27 48 13 93 55 34 18 37 79 49 90
```

```
20 69 22 40 98 27 37 83 28 71 69 62 03 42 73 00 06 41 41 74 45 89 09 39 84
40 23 72 51 39 10 65 81 92 59 73 42 37 11 61 58 76 17 14 97 04 76 62 16 17
73 96 53 97 86 59 71 74 17 32 64 63 91 08 25 27 55 10 24 19 23 71 82 13 74
38 26 61 70 04 33 73 99 19 87 95 60 78 46 75 26 72 39 27 67 53 77 57 68 93
48 67 26 43 18 87 14 77 43 96 99 17 43 48 76 43 00 65 98 50 45 60 33 01 07
55 03 36 67 68 72 87 08 62 40 24 62 01 61 16 16 06 10 89 20 23 21 34 74 97
44 10 13 85 57 73 96 07 94 52 19 59 50 88 92 09 65 90 77 47 25 76 16 19 33
95 06 79 88 54 79 96 23 53 10 48 03 45 15 22 65 39 07 16 29 45 33 02 43 70
68 15 54 35 02 42 35 48 96 32 95 33 95 22 00 18 74 72 00 18 22 85 61 68 90
58 42 36 72 24 58 37 52 18 51 90 84 60 79 80 24 36 59 87 38 67 80 43 79 33
95 67 47 29 83 94 69 40 06 07 46 40 62 98 82 54 97 20 56 95 27 62 50 96 72
98 57 07 23 69 65 95 39 69 58 20 31 89 03 43 38 46 82 68 72 33 78 80 87 15
56 69 47 07 41 90 22 91 07 12 71 59 73 05 50 08 22 23 71 77 13 13 92 66 99
```

Source: F. C. Powell, *Cambridge Mathematical and Statistical Tables* (Cambridge: Cambridge University Press, 1976), p. 55. Reproduced by permission of the publisher.

Appendix 3 Z-scores table

To find out what proportion of scores lies between your score and the mean score, or what proportion of scores is higher or lower than yours, use this table. For example, for a score with a z-value of 1.5 (or −1.5), 43.32% of scores in the set separate it from the mean. Equally, for a score with a z-value of 1.55 (or −1.5), 43.94% of scores separate it from the mean; therefore 43.94% of scores are higher than that score.

z	0.00	0.01	0.02	0.03	0.04	0.05	0.06	0.07	0.08	0.09
0.0	00.00	00.40	00.80	01.20	01.60	01.99	02.39	02.79	03.19	03.59
0.1	03.98	04.38	04.78	05.17	05.57	05.96	06.36	06.75	07.14	07.53
0.2	07.93	08.32	08.71	09.10	09.48	09.87	10.26	10.64	11.03	11.41
0.3	11.79	12.17	12.55	12.93	13.31	13.68	14.06	14.43	14.80	15.17
0.4	15.54	15.91	16.28	16.64	17.00	17.36	17.72	18.08	18.44	18.79
0.5	19.15	19.50	19.85	20.19	20.54	20.88	21.23	21.57	21.90	22.24
0.6	22.57	22.91	23.24	23.57	23.89	24.22	24.54	24.86	25.17	25.49
0.7	25.80	26.11	26.42	26.73	27.04	27.34	27.64	27.94	28.23	28.52
0.8	28.81	29.10	29.39	29.67	29.95	30.23	30.51	30.78	31.06	31.33
0.9	31.59	31.86	32.12	32.38	32.64	32.89	33.15	33.40	33.65	33.89
1.0	34.13	34.38	34.61	34.85	35.08	35.31	35.54	35.77	35.99	36.21
1.1	36.43	36.65	36.86	37.08	37.29	37.49	37.70	37.90	38.10	38.30
1.2	38.49	38.69	38.88	39.07	39.25	39.44	39.62	39.80	39.97	40.15
1.3	40.32	40.49	40.66	40.82	40.99	41.15	41.31	41.47	41.62	41.77
1.4	41.92	42.07	42.22	42.36	42.51	42.65	42.79	42.92	43.06	43.19
1.5	43.32	43.45	43.57	43.70	43.82	43.94	44.06	44.18	44.29	44.41
1.6	44.52	44.63	44.74	44.84	44.95	45.05	45.15	45.25	45.35	45.45
1.7	45.54	45.64	45.73	45.82	45.91	45.99	46.08	46.16	46.25	46.33
1.8	46.41	46.49	46.56	46.64	46.71	46.78	46.86	46.93	46.99	47.06
1.9	47.13	47.19	47.26	47.32	47.38	47.44	47.50	47.56	47.61	47.67
2.0	47.72	47.78	47.83	47.88	47.93	47.98	48.03	48.08	48.12	48.17
2.1	48.21	48.26	48.30	48.34	48.38	48.42	48.46	48.50	48.54	48.57
2.2	48.61	48.64	48.68	48.71	48.75	48.78	48.81	48.84	48.87	48.90
2.3	48.93	48.96	48.98	49.01	49.04	49.06	49.09	49.11	49.13	49.16
2.4	49.18	49.20	49.22	49.25	49.27	49.29	49.31	49.32	49.34	49.36
2.5	49.38	49.40	49.41	49.43	49.45	49.46	49.48	49.49	49.51	49.52
2.6	49.53	49.55	49.56	49.57	49.59	49.60	49.61	49.62	49.63	49.64
2.7	49.65	49.66	49.67	49.68	49.69	49.70	49.71	49.72	49.73	49.74
2.8	49.74	49.75	49.76	49.77	49.77	49.78	49.79	49.79	49.80	49.81
2.9	49.81	49.82	49.82	49.83	49.84	49.84	49.85	49.85	49.86	49.86
3.0	49.87	49.87	49.87	49.88	49.88	49.89	49.89	49.89	49.90	49.90

Source: F. C. Powell, *Cambridge Mathematical and Statistical Tables* (Cambridge: Cambridge University Press, 1976), p. 71. Reproduced by permission of the publisher.

Appendix 4 Test of goodness of fit

To find out if a given set of scores approximates to the ideal, normally distributed set, use this **goodness of fit test**. To begin the test, say you have a set of scores plotted on a histogram as follows:

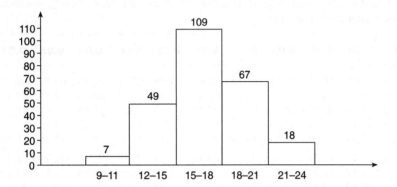

There are 250 scores in this set. The mean value for the set is 17 and standard deviation (*SD*) is 2.7. Here's how to carry out a **goodness of fit test** on this set of scores.

Step 1 Work out the 'predicted' histogram frequencies as though the set was normally distributed. Do this by working out the 'predicted' proportion of scores lying in each interval along the horizontal axis of the histogram.

In our example, the first interval lies between the values 9 and 12.
9 is $(17 - 9) \div 2.7$ *SDs* = 2.96 *SDs* away from the mean value.
12 is $(17 - 12) \div 2.7$ *SDs* = 1.85 *SDs* away from the mean.

The 'predicted' proportion of scores between 9 and 12 is $49.85 - 46.78 = 3\%$ (to the nearest %).

These values are taken from the table in Appendix 3, using procedures described in Appendix 3. Now, repeating this calculation for all the intervals along the horizontal axis: 20% of scores lie between 12 and 15, 41% lie between 15 and 18, 29% lie between 18 and 21, and 7% lie between 21 and 24.

Step 2 Work out the 'predicted' frequency of scores in each interval. Do this by multiplying the proportions found in *step 1* by N (the total number of scores).

In our example, the outcomes of these calculations, in ascending order, are as follows:

7.5 (between 9 and 12), 50 (12 to 15), 102.5 (15 to 18), 72.5 (18 to 21), 17.5 (21 to 24)

Step 3 For each interval, work out:
(the observed frequency – the 'predicted' frequency)^2 ÷ (the 'predicted' frequency)

In our example, these calculations are:

$(7 - 7.5)^2 ÷ 7.5$, $(49 - 50)^2 ÷ 50$, $(109 - 102.5)^2 ÷ 102.5$, $(67 - 72.5)^2 ÷ 72.5$, $(18 - 17.5)^2 ÷ 17.5$
which yields the values 0.033, 0.02, 0.412, 0.417, 0.014.

Step 4 Work out the sum of the outcomes of step 3 to find D.
In our example, $D = 0.033 + 0.02 + 0.412 + 0.417 + 0.014$ $D = 0.896$

Step 5 Count the number of intervals along the horizontal axis of your histogram to find k. Subtract 3 from the value of k, to find df (degrees of freedom).
In our example, $k = 5$, and so $df = 2$

Step 6 Look up the critical value of χ^2 in the table below for the corresponding df value. For there to be a significant difference between the actual distribution and the normal model at the 95% level, D must be greater than the value in the table.

In our example, D, 0.896, is less than the critical value in the table, 4.605, so we can assume a normal model at the 95% level.

df	critical value of χ^2
1	2.706
2	4.605
3	6.251
4	7.779
5	9.236
6	10.64
7	12.02
8	13.36
9	14.68

df	*critical value of* χ^2
10	15.99
11	17.28
12	18.55
13	19.81
14	21.06
15	22.31
16	23.54
17	24.77
18	25.99
19	27.2
20	28.41

Source: F. C. Powell, *Cambridge Mathematical and Statistical Tables* (Cambridge: Cambridge University Press, 1976), p. 75. Reproduced by permission of the publisher.

Appendix 5   Ranking a set of scores

This involves assigning every value in a set a 'rank score'. In other words, putting them in order, from first to last. It's the convention to give the smallest value the rank of 1 and the largest value the rank of N, N being equal to the number of values in a set. Generally it's a pretty straightforward procedure, with minor complications where you have values that appear in a set more than once. Steps 3 and 4 below should straighten out some of these complications. Here's how you'd rank this set: 1, 3, 4, 4, 6, 6, 6, 7, 7, 7, 7, 9.

Step 1   Arrange the set in a column, with the smallest value at the head, the largest at the foot:

scores	preliminary rank scores	final rank scores
1	(1)	(1)
3	(2)	(2)
4	(3)	(3.5)
4	(4)	(3.5)
6	(5)	(6)
6	(6)	(6)
6	(7)	(6)
7	(8)	(9.5)
7	(9)	(9.5)
7	(10)	(9.5)
7	(11)	(9.5)
9	(12)	(12)

Step 2   Allocate **preliminary rank scores**. Do this by giving the top value a score of 1, the next value down a score of 2 and so on until you reach the bottom value, which gets a score of N. (N being equal to the number of values in the set). In step 1, preliminary rank scores are shown in the middle column, in brackets.

Step 3   Look for **tied values**. Do this by casting your eye down the set to see if any values appear more than once. In our example there are three tied values – 4 (appearing twice), 6 (appearing three times) and 7 (appearing four times). If your set has no tied values, accept your preliminary rank scores as final rank scores. If your set does have ties, go to step 4.

Step 4 Allocate **final rank scores**. Do this by giving each tied value the 'middle preliminary rank score' for that tie. So for example, for the tied value of 6 (whose three preliminary rank scores are 5, 6 and 7) the middle preliminary rank score is 6. Therefore all these three values take the final rank score of 6. For the tied value of 4, whose preliminary rank scores are 3 and 4, there is no middle preliminary rank score, so these two values take a final rank score that's half way between the two preliminary rank scores. So they take the final rank score of 3.5. It's worth noting that whenever there's a tie between an even number of values the final rank scores will always be 'something and a half'. In step 1, final rank scores are shown in the right-hand column.

Appendix 6   The F-test

Testing for similarity of dispersion between two sets of scores calls for what's known as the **F-test**, or Variance Ratio test. Use the F-test when you have two sets of scores at the interval level of measurement. Here's how you'd do an F-test on sets A and B, shown below:

	Set A	Set B	Set A²	Set B²
	2	4	4	16
	3	5	9	25
	4	5	16	25
	4	6	16	36
	5	6	25	36
	5	7	25	49
	5	7	25	49
	6	8	36	64
	7	10	49	100
	9	11	81	121
Totals	**50**	**69**	**286**	**521**

Step 1   Calculate the mean values for *set A* and *set B*:
    Set A mean = $(2 + 3 + 4 + 4 + 5 + 5 + 5 + 6 + 7 + 9) \div 10 = 5$ Set A mean = 5
    Set B mean = $(4 + 5 + 5 + 6 + 6 + 7 + 7 + 8 + 10 + 11) \div 10 = 6.9$
    Set B mean = 6.9

Step 2   Square the *set A* total, then divide by N_A: Square the *set B* total, then divide by N_B:
    $50^2 \div 10 = 250$ $69^2 \div 10 = 476.1$

Step 3   Subtract the outcomes of step 2 from the *set A²* and *set B²* totals:
    $286 - 250 = 36$ $521 - 476.1 = 44.9$

Step 4   Divide the outcomes of step 3 by N-1 to find the variance for *sets A* and *B*:
    $36 \div 9 = 4$ *variance A* = 4 $44.9 \div 9 = 4.99$ *variance B* = 4.99

Step 5 Divide the larger variance by the smaller, to find F:

$4.99 \div 4 = 1.3 \quad F = 1.25$

Step 6 To find out if there is similarity of dispersion between the two sets of scores, use the table below. To use this table, find the appropriate intersecting value of F as follows. Look along *row N* until you reach the value of $N - 1$ for the set of scores with the larger variance. Next, look down *column N* until you reach the value of $N -!$ for the set of scores with the smaller variance. If your value for F is **smaller than** the appropriate intersecting value of F, you can conclude (with 95% certainty) that there is similarity of dispersion between your two sets.

Row *N*

	1	2	3	4	5	6	7	8	9	10	12	15	20	24	30	40	60	120	∞
1	648	800	864	900	922	937	948	957	963	969	977	985	993	997	1001	1006	1010	1014	1018
2	38.51	39.00	39.16	39.25	39.30	39.33	39.36	39.37	39.39	39.40	39.42	39.43	39.45	39.46	39.46	39.47	39.48	39.49	39.50
3	17.44	16.04	15.44	15.10	14.88	14.74	14.62	14.54	14.47	14.42	14.34	14.25	14.17	14.12	14.08	14.04	13.99	13.95	13.90
4	12.22	10.65	9.98	9.60	9.36	9.20	9.07	8.98	8.90	8.84	8.75	8.66	8.56	8.51	8.46	8.41	8.36	8.31	8.26
5	10.01	8.43	7.76	7.39	7.15	6.98	6.85	6.76	6.68	6.62	6.52	6.43	6.33	6.28	6.23	6.18	6.12	6.07	6.02
6	8.81	7.26	6.60	6.23	5.99	5.82	5.70	5.60	5.52	5.46	5.37	5.27	5.17	5.12	5.07	5.01	4.96	4.90	4.85
7	8.07	6.54	5.89	5.52	5.29	5.12	4.99	4.90	4.82	4.76	4.67	4.57	4.47	4.42	4.36	4.31	4.25	4.20	4.14
8	7.57	6.06	5.42	5.05	4.82	4.65	4.53	4.43	4.36	4.30	4.20	4.10	4.00	3.95	3.89	3.84	3.78	3.73	3.67
9	7.21	5.71	5.08	4.72	4.48	4.32	4.20	4.10	4.03	3.96	3.87	3.77	3.67	3.61	3.56	3.51	3.45	3.39	3.33
10	6.94	5.46	4.83	4.47	4.24	4.07	3.95	3.85	3.78	3.72	3.62	3.52	3.42	3.37	3.31	3.26	3.20	3.14	3.08
12	6.55	5.10	4.47	4.12	3.89	3.73	3.61	3.51	3.44	3.37	3.28	3.18	3.07	3.02	2.96	2.91	2.85	2.79	2.72
15	6.20	4.76	4.15	3.80	3.58	3.41	3.29	3.20	3.12	3.06	2.96	2.86	2.76	2.70	2.64	2.58	2.52	2.46	2.40
20	5.87	4.46	3.86	3.51	3.29	3.13	3.01	2.91	2.84	2.77	2.68	2.57	2.46	2.41	2.35	2.29	2.22	2.16	2.09
24	5.72	4.32	3.72	3.38	3.15	2.99	2.87	2.78	2.70	2.64	2.54	2.44	2.33	2.27	2.21	2.15	2.08	2.01	1.94
30	5.57	4.18	3.59	3.25	3.03	2.87	2.75	2.65	2.57	2.51	2.41	2.31	2.20	2.14	2.07	2.01	1.94	1.87	1.79
40	5.42	4.05	3.46	3.13	2.90	2.74	2.62	2.53	2.45	2.39	2.29	2.18	2.07	2.01	1.94	1.88	1.80	1.72	1.64
60	5.29	3.93	3.34	3.01	2.79	2.63	2.51	2.41	2.33	2.27	2.17	2.06	1.94	1.88	1.82	1.74	1.67	1.58	1.48
120	5.15	3.80	3.23	2.89	2.67	2.52	2.39	2.30	2.22	2.16	2.05	1.94	1.82	1.76	1.69	1.61	1.53	1.43	1.31
∞	5.02	3.69	3.12	2.79	2.57	2.41	2.29	2.19	2.11	2.05	1.94	1.83	1.71	1.64	1.57	1.48	1.39	1.27	1.00

Appendix 7 Sign test table

To find out if the result of your **Sign test** is significant at the 5 per cent level, consult the table below. To be significant at the 5 per cent level, your value of S must be **equal to or less than** the value in the table, for the appropriate value of N.

N	For a two-tailed hypothesis	For a one-tailed hypothesis
5	–	0
6	0	0
7	0	0
8	0	1
9	1	1
10	1	1
11	1	2
12	2	2
13	2	3
14	2	3
15	3	3
16	3	4
17	4	4
18	4	5
19	4	5
20	5	5
25	7	7
30	9	10
35	11	12

Source: Frances Clegg, *Simple Statistics* (Cambridge: Cambridge University Press, 1990) p. 163. Reproduced with permission of the publisher.

If your value of S is **equal to or less than** the value shown in the table, you can reject your null hypothesis and declare your result significant at the 5 per cent level.

Appendix 8   Chi-square test table

To find out if the result of your **chi-square test** is significant at the 5 per cent level, consult the table below. To be significant at the 5 percent level, your value of χ^2 must be **equal to or more than** the value in the table.

For a two-tailed hypothesis	For a one-tailed hypothesis
3.841	2.706

Source: F. C. Powell, *Cambridge Mathematical and Statistical Tables* (Cambridge: Cambridge University Press, 1976), p. 73. Reproduced with permission of the publisher.

If your value of χ^2 is **equal to or more than** the value in the table, you can reject your null hypothesis and declare your result significant at the 5 per cent level. This table should only be used where your data is set out in a simple 2 × 2 table in step 1 of the calculation. More complex versions of this test use a different version of this inferential test – the Complex chi-square.

Appendix 9   Wilcoxon test table

To find out if the result of your **Wilcoxon test** is significant at the 5 per cent level, consult the table below. To be significant at the 5 per cent level, your value of T must be **equal to or less than** the value in the table.

N	For a two-tailed hypothesis	For a one-tailed hypothesis
5	–	1
6	1	2
7	2	4
8	4	6
9	6	8
10	8	11
11	11	14
12	14	17
13	17	21
14	21	26
15	25	30
16	30	36
17	35	41
18	40	47
19	46	54
20	52	60
21	59	68
22	66	75
23	73	83
24	81	92
25	90	101
26	98	110
27	107	120
28	117	130
29	127	141
30	137	152
31	148	163
32	159	175
33	171	188
34	183	201
35	195	214
36	208	228
37	222	242
38	235	256
39	250	271

N	For a two-tailed hypothesis	For a one-tailed hypothesis
40	264	287
41	279	303
42	295	319
43	311	336
44	327	353
45	343	371
46	361	389
47	379	408
48	397	427
49	415	446
50	434	466

If your value of T is **equal to or less than** the value in the table, you can reject your null hypothesis and declare your result significant at the 5 per cent level.

Appendix 10   Mann–Whitney U-test table

To find out if your value for the **Mann–Whitney U-test** is significant at the 5 per cent level, use the table below. To be significant your value of U *must not exceed* the value in the table for the appropriate value of *NA* and *NB*. Note that the values in the table apply to *two-tailed hypotheses* at the 5 per cent significance level.

NB values

	1	2	3	4	5	6	7	8	9	10	11	12	13	14	15	16	17	18	19	20
1	–	–	–	–	–	–	–	–	–	–	–	–	–	–	–	–	–	–	–	–
2	–	–	–	–	–	–	–	0	0	0	0	1	1	1	1	1	2	2	2	2
3	–	–	–	–	0	1	1	2	2	3	3	4	4	5	5	6	6	7	7	8
4	–	–	–	0	1	2	3	4	4	5	6	7	8	9	1	11	11	12	13	14
5	–	–	0	1	2	3	5	6	7	8	9	11	12	13	14	15	17	18	19	20
6	–	–	1	2	3	5	6	8	10	11	13	14	16	17	19	21	22	24	25	27
7	–	–	1	3	5	6	8	10	12	14	16	18	20	22	24	26	28	30	32	34
8	–	0	2	4	6	8	10	13	15	17	19	22	24	26	29	31	34	36	38	41
9	–	0	2	4	7	10	12	15	17	20	23	26	28	31	34	37	39	42	45	48
10	–	0	3	5	8	11	14	17	20	23	26	29	33	36	39	42	45	48	52	55
11	–	0	3	6	9	13	16	19	23	25	30	33	37	40	44	47	51	55	58	62
12	–	1	4	7	11	14	18	22	26	29	33	37	41	45	49	53	57	61	65	69
13	–	1	4	8	12	16	20	24	28	33	37	41	45	50	54	59	63	67	72	76
14	–	1	5	9	13	17	22	26	31	36	40	45	50	55	56	64	69	74	78	83
15	–	1	5	10	14	19	24	29	34	39	44	49	54	59	64	70	75	80	85	90
16	–	1	6	11	15	21	26	31	37	42	47	53	59	64	70	75	81	86	92	98
17	–	2	6	11	17	22	28	34	39	45	51	57	63	69	75	81	87	93	99	105
18	–	2	7	12	18	24	30	36	42	48	55	61	67	74	80	86	93	99	106	112
19	–	2	7	13	19	25	32	38	45	52	58	65	72	78	85	92	99	106	113	119
20	–	2	8	14	20	27	34	41	48	55	62	69	76	83	90	98	105	112	119	127

(left axis: NA values)

Source: Joan G. Snodgrass, *The Numbers Came* (London: Oxford University Press, 1978). Reproduced by permission of the publisher).

If your value of U is *equal to or less than* the value in the table for the appropriate values of *NA* and *NB*, reject your null hypothesis and declare your result significant at the 5 per cent level.

Appendix 11 The *t*-test table

To find out if the result of your **t-test** is significant at the 5 per cent level, consult the table below. To be significant at the 5 per cent level, your value of *t* must be *equal to or more than* the value in the table. If the *t* value for the precise *df* you're using isn't included in the table, use the nearest possible value. So if *df* = 38, use *df* = 40. To be significant, if your value of *t* is *equal to or more than* the value in the table, reject your null hypothesis and declare your result significant at the 5 per cent level.

df	For a two-tailed hypothesis	For a one-tailed hypothesis
1	12.71	6.314
2	4.303	2.920
3	3.182	2.353
4	2.776	2.132
5	2.571	2.015
6	2.447	1.943
7	2.365	1.895
8	2.306	1.860
9	2.262	1.833
10	2.228	1.812
11	2.201	1.796
12	2.179	1.782
13	2.160	1.771
14	2.145	1.761
15	2.131	1.753
16	2.120	1.746
17	2.110	1.740
18	2.101	1.734
19	2.093	1.729
20	2.086	1.725
21	2.080	1.721
22	2.074	1.717
23	2.069	1.714
24	2.064	1.711
25	2.060	1.708
26	2.056	1.706
27	2.052	1.703
28	2.048	1.701
29	2.045	1.699
30	2.042	1.697

df	For a two-tailed hypothesis	For a one-tailed hypothesis
40	2.021	1.684
60	2	1.671
120	1.980	1.658
240	1.960	1.645

Source: F. C. Powell, *Cambridge Mathematical and Statistical Tables* (Cambridge: Cambridge University Press, 1976), p. 72. Reproduced by permission of the publisher.

Appendix 12   Pearson's product-moment table

To find out if the result of your **Pearson's product-moment calculation** is significant at the 5 per cent level, consult the table below. For significance at the 5 per cent level, your value of r must be *equal to or more than* the one in the table.

N-2	For a two-tailed hypothesis	For a one-tailed hypothesis
2	0.95	0.9
3	0.878	0.805
4	0.811	0.729
5	0.754	0.669
6	0.707	0.621
7	0.666	0.582
8	0.632	0.549
9	0.602	0.521
10	0.576	0.497
11	0.553	0.476
12	0.532	0.457
13	0.514	0.441
14	0.497	0.426
15	0.482	0.412
16	0.468	0.4
17	0.456	0.389
18	0.444	0.378
19	0.433	0.369
20	0.423	0.36
25	0.381	0.323
30	0.349	0.296
35	0.325	0.275
40	0.304	0.257
45	0.288	0.243
50	0.273	0.231
60	0.25	0.211
70	0.232	0.195
80	0.217	0.183
90	0.205	0.173
100	0.195	0.164

Source: F. C. Powell, *Cambridge Mathematical and Statistical Tables* (Cambridge: Cambridge University Press, 1976), p. 69. Reproduced by permission of the publisher.

If your value of r is *equal to or more than* the one in the table for the appropriate value of N-2, reject your null hypothesis and declare your result significant at the 5 per cent level.

Appendix 13   Spearman's rho table

To find out if the result of your Spearman's rho calculation is significant at the 5 per cent level, consult the table below. For significance at the 5 per cent level, your value of rho must be *equal to or more than* the one in the table for the appropriate value of N (the number of pairs of scores).

N	For a two-tailed hypothesis	For a one-tailed hypothesis
5	1	0.9
6	0.886	0.829
7	0.786	0.714
8	0.738	0.643
9	0.683	0.6
10	0.648	0.564
12	0.591	0.506
14	0.544	0.456
16	0.506	0.425
18	0.475	0.399
20	0.45	0.377
22	0.428	0.359
24	0.409	0.343
26	0.392	0.329
28	0.377	0.317
30	0.364	0.306

Source: J. G. Snodgrass, *The Numbers Game* (London: Oxford University Press, 1978), table C6. Reproduced by permission of the publisher.

If your value of rho is *equal to or more than* the appropriate value in the table, reject your null hypothesis and declare your result significant at the 5 per cent level.

References

American Psychiatric Association (1980), *Diagnostic and Statistical Manual of Mental Disorders*, 3rd edn (Washington, DC: American Psychiatric Association).

Bales, R. (1958), 'Task Roles and Social Roles in Problem-solving Groups', in Maccoby, E. (ed.), *Readings in Social Psychology*, 3rd edn (New York: Holt, Rinehart and Winston).

Banyard, P. (1998), *Applying Psychology to Health* (London: Hodder & Stoughton).

Banyard, P. and Grayson, A. (1996), *Introducing Psychological Research* (Basingstoke: Macmillan – now Palgrave).

Bell, J. (1989), *Doing your Research Project* (Milton Keynes, Bucks: Open University).

Bell, P., Fisher, J., Baum, A. and Greene, T. (1996), *Environmental Psychology* (New York: Harcourt Brace).

Bilton, T. *et al.* (1996), *Introductory Sociology*, 3rd edn (Basingstoke: Macmillan – now Palgrave).

British Psychological Society (1985), 'Guidelines for the Use of Animals in Research', *Bulletin of the BPS*, **38**, 289–91.

British Psychological Society (1995), *Ethical Principles for Conducting Research with Human Participants* (Leicester: British Psychological Society).

Buzan, T. (1995), *Use Your Head* (London: BBC Books).

Carbo, R., Dunn, R. and Dunn, K. (1986), *Teaching Students through their Individual Learning Styles* (Englewood Cliffs, NJ: Prentice-Hall).

Clegg, F. (1990), *Simple Statistics* (Cambridge: Cambridge University Press).

Coolican, H. (1996), *Introduction to Research Methods and Statistics in Psychology* (London: Hodder & Stoughton).

Coolican, H. (1999), *Research Methods and Statistics in Psychology*, 3rd edn (London: Hodder & Stoughton).

Dunn, R., Dunn, K. and Price, G. (1985), *Learning Styles Inventory* (Lawrence, KS: Price Systems).

Dyer, C. (1995), *Beginning Research in Psychology* (Oxford: Blackwell).

Entwistle, N. (1981), *Styles of Learning and Teaching* (Chichester: John Wiley).

Erikson, E. (1980), *Identity and the Life Cycle* (New York: W. W. Norton).

Finnigan, D. (1992), *The Complete Juggler* (Bath: Butterfingers).

Foster, J. and Parker, I. (1995), *Carrying out Investigations in Psychology* (Leicester: British Psychological Society).

Freud, S. (1909), 'Analysis of a Phobia of a Five-Year Old Boy', in *The Pelican Freud Library* (1977), vol. 8: *Case Histories*, 1, pp. 169–306.

Freud, S. (1913), *The Complete Psychological Works of Sigmund Freud*, vol. 13 ed. J. Strachey (London: Hogarth Press).

Gross, R. D. (1994), *Key Studies in Psychology* (London: Hodder & Stoughton).

Gross, R. D. (1997), *Psychology: The Science of Mind and Behaviour* (London: Hodder and Stoughton).

Gross, R. and McIlveen, R. (1999), *Perspectives in Psychology* (London: Hodder & Stoughton).

Haworth, J. (ed.) (1996), *Psychological Research: Innovative Methods and Strategies* (London: Routledge & Kegan Paul).

Heffernan, T. (1997), *A Student's Guide to Studying Psychology* (Hove: Psychology Press).

Hiatt, L. R. (1996), *Arguments about Aboriginals* (Cambridge: Cambridge University Press).

Homans, G. C. (1974), *Social Behaviour: Its Elementary Forms*, 2nd edn (New York: Harcourt Brace Janovich).

Koestler, A. (1970), *The Ghost in the Machine* (London: Pan).

Lapiere, R. (1934), 'Attitudes vs. actions', *Social Forces*, **13**, 230–7.

Malim, T. and Birch, A. (1998), *Introductory Psychology* (Basingstoke: Macmillan – now Palgrave).

Malinowski, B. (1950), *Argonauts of the Western Pacific* (London: Routledge & Kegan Paul; first edition 1922).

May, T. (1993), *Social Research* (Buckingham: Open University Press).

Meyer, P. (1970), *Introductory Probability and Statistical Applications*, 2nd edn (Reading, MA: Addison-Wesley).

Meyerwitz, B. E. and Chaiken, S. (1987), 'The Effect of Message Framing on Breast Self-examination Attitudes, Intentions and Behaviour', *Journal of Personality and Social Psychology*, **52**, 500–10.

Milgram, S. (1963), 'Behavioural Study of Obedience', *Journal of Abnormal and Social Psychology*, **67**, 371–8.

Mumford, A. (1993), 'Putting Learning Styles to Work: an Integrated Approach', *Journal of European Industrial Training*, **17**(10), 3–9.

Powell, F. (1976), *Cambridge Mathematical and Statistical Tables* (Cambridge: Cambridge University Press).

Riding, R. J. (1991), *Cognitive Styles Analysis* (Birmingham: Learning and Training Technology).

Riding, R. and Cheemal, I. (1991), 'Cognitive Styles: an Overview', *Educational Psychology*, **11** (3 and 4), pp. 193–215.

Rose, C. (1986), *Accelerated Learning* (Aylesbury: Accelerated Learning Systems).

Rosenhan, D. (1973), 'On being Sane in Insane Places', *Science*, **179**, 250–8.

Sacks, O. (1985), *The Man Who Mistook his Wife for a Hat* (London: Picador).

Sadler-Smith, E. (1996), 'Learning Styles: a Holistic Approach', *Journal of European Industrial Training*, **20**(7), 29–36.

Snodgrass, J. (1978), *The Numbers Game* (London: Oxford University Press).

Sommer, B. and Sommer, R. (1991), *A Practical Guide to Behavioural Research* (Oxford: Oxford University Press).

Tomkinson, B. (1999), *Learning in Style* (Manchester: Enterprise Centre for Learning and Curriculum, Innovation, UMIST).

Wadely, A. (1991), *Ethics in Psychological Research and Practice* (Leicester: British Psychological Society).

Wolpe, J. and Rachman, S. (1960), 'Psychoanalytic Evidence: a Critique Based on Freud's Case of Little Hans', *Journal of Nervous and Mental Disease*, **131**, 135–45.

Zimbardo, P. (1988), *Psychology and Life*, 12th edn (Glenview, IL: Scott Foresman).

Index